S0-BND-627

Ken Russell

edited by
Thomas R. Atkins

MONARCH PRESS

Standard Book Number 671-08102-0

Library of Congress Catalog Card Number: 75-23545

Designed by Denise Biller

Published by
MONARCH PRESS
a division of Simon & Schuster, Inc.
1 West 39th Street
New York, N.Y. 10018

CONTENTS

CONTRIBUTORS

THOMAS R. ATKINS, Chairman of the Theatre Arts Department at Hollins College, Virginia, is Editor-Publisher of *The Film Journal* and author of *Sexuality in the Movies*.

JOHN BAXTER, a London critic, is the author of *Science Fiction in the Cinema; Stunt: The Story of the Great Movie Stunt Men; An Appalling Talent: Ken Russell;* and *Beyond the Fragile Geometry of Space.*

JACK FISHER, who teaches film and theater at Norfolk State College in Virginia, has published criticism in *The Film Journal, Contempora,* and other magazines.

JOSEPH A. GOMEZ, a teacher at Mohawk Valley Community College in Utica, New York, has written for *Film Heritage, Literature/ Film Quarterly,* and *The Journal of Popular Film.*

GENE D. PHILLIPS, S.J., teaches fiction and film at Loyola University of Chicago and is the author of *The Movie Makers: Artists in an Industry* and *Graham Greene: The Films of His Fiction.*

ACKNOWLEDGMENTS

Ken and Shirley Russell were especially helpful in the assembling of this volume. The editor is grateful to both for taking time out for long conversations about their work and for special screenings of several of Russell's films.

The editor also wishes to thank John Baxter for making useful suggestions about the manuscript and for providing many of the photographs. His book, *An Appalling Talent: Ken Russell,* is the basis for many of the biographical details and quotes used in *Ballet Fantastique.*

Jack Fisher's article appeared originally in *The Film Journal,* Volume II, Number 1.

Photographs are courtesy of the following sources: Gene D. Phillips, Joseph A. Gomez, BBC-TV, United Artists, Warner Brothers, MGM-EMI, Goodtimes Enterprises, Robert Stigwood Productions, and the Stills Archive of the British Film Institute.

The excerpts from the screenplays of *Mahler* and *Tommy* are courtesy of Ken Russell and are reprinted with his permission.

Ken Russell on location for **Mahler**

PREFACE

What are dreams? A random sequence of scenes, trivial or tragic, viatic or static, fantastic or familiar, featuring more or less plausible events patched up with grotesque details, and recasting dead people in new settings.
— Vladimir Nabokov, *Ada*

The dreamlike, imagistic, intensely personal films of Ken Russell have made him one of the best-known of all contemporary directors. He is also among the most controversial, largely because of his aggressive assault on viewers' sensibilities and unabashed use of eroticism and violence in his art. Russell's current fame as the *enfant terrible* of British cinema was preceded by an extraordinary career as a television director for BBC-TV during the sixties. Using actors to portray living and dead artists, he made a series of experimental films, such as *Isadora Duncan, The Biggest Dancer in the World; Dante's Inferno* (about the painter Dante Gabriel Rossetti); and *Dance of the Seven Veils: A Comic Strip in Seven Episodes on the Life of Richard Strauss,* which revolutionized and revitalized the concept of the biographical documentary.

Russell in 1968

Russell directing school children in **Isadora Duncan**

Like many Americans, I first became aware of Ken Russell in 1969 with the release of his *Women in Love*, a bold D. H. Lawrence adaptation that solidly established his reputation as a director of international importance. In 1972, while spending several months in London on a writing project, I saw his next three features — *The Music Lovers, The Devils,* and *The Boy Friend* — all running simultaneously in the West End, an unprecedented event in British film history. A year later, through the critic John Baxter, I met Russell and his wife Shirley, an imaginative designer who does the costumes for his films.

Filming a scene for **Dante's Inferno** *with Oliver Reed and Judith Paris*

Russell directing Oliver Reed and Vanessa Redgrave in **The Devils**

This book resulted from additional meetings with Russell, an extremely generous and friendly person despite his wild press image, and from numerous viewings of his films, many of which have been either hysterically dismissed or totally misinterpreted by critics. The majority of contributors to this volume know Russell and write from first-hand experience of his working methods and intentions. The essays cover his entire career, from the early amateur shorts through the television bio-pics to his remarkable features.

Mahler, Russell's eighth feature, opens with a stunning image that is typical not only of his work but of his nature as an artist. We see a long shot of a small hut beside a beautiful mountain lake. As the camera slowly zooms in on this deceptively idyllic scene, the hut suddenly bursts into raging flames. The exploding of the lakeside hut, a retreat where Gustav Mahler did some of his com-

Coaching a family scene in **Mahler**

posing, is a metaphoric event — an image of the composer's fiery creativity as well as the inferno of his emotional life. It also undercuts the audience's expectations and provides a warning that this film is not the standard sentimental, romanticized portrait of the musician. Instead of focusing on exterior historical details, *Mahler* offers a haunting, phantasmagorical exploration of the artist's inner turmoil which found vivid expression in his music.

Russell's complex, combustible mixture of sacred and profane elements, high and low art, makes his films popular with audiences but difficult to analyze verbally or categorize. His best work combines the graphic immediacy and simplicity of the comic strip with the subtlety and suggestiveness of music.

After talking with Russell about *The Devils* and several of his other films, my wife Mary Ellen and I mentioned the near impossibility of trying to label or sum up the phenomenal richness and emotional power of his work. Russell suggested that we do an "interpretation," as he has done with other artists — a personal impression based on our individual reactions and ideas. This book then is one such interpretation, using material as varied as an imaginary film scenario, factual reporting, close critical analysis, and excerpts from Russell's scripts. Hopefully, it will lead readers to their own interpretation and enjoyment of a unique artist.

Filming of Pinball Wizard sequence from **Tommy**

BALLET FANTASTIQUE:
SCENARIO FOR AN IMAGINARY BIO-PIC OF KEN RUSSELL

Thomas R. Atkins

Et puis ce soir on s'en ira
Au cinéma

Les Artistes que sont-ce donc
Ce ne sont plus ceux qui cultivent les Beaux-Arts . . .

Aussi mon Dieu faut-il avoir du goût
> — *Apollinaire*
> *"Avant le Cinéma"*[1]

---

[1]And then tonight we will go
To the movies
These artists, what are they?
They are no longer those who cultivate the Fine Arts . . .
Therefore, for goodness sake, it is essential to have some taste
> — "At the Movies"
> free translation

I. Title: CHILDHOOD

1. Close-up of a large poster showing King Kong on the Empire State Building clutching Fay Wray in his paw. Reverse zoom to reveal Russell as a small boy dressed in a sailor suit standing beneath the poster. He reaches up toward Kong. Thunder and lightning. Music from thirties horror movies. The gorilla's eyes roll and peer down at the boy.

2. Long shot of forbidding old house in Southampton. Camera tracks around side of house and up driveway to ominous garage. Dissolve to dark interior of garage where the boy in the sailor suit is pounding on the door. Sound of loud breath-

Open-air stage at Larmer Tree Gardens where scene was filmed but not used in **The Music Lovers**

ing behind him. He turns, terrified. The huge face of Kong appears in the darkness. The beast passes a motion picture projector to the boy. Handel's *Messiah* is heard. Iris out on Kong.

3. Fade in on long shot of procession of Riley automobiles winding along coast and into a spacious park with an open-air stage. The park scenery resembles a Maxfield Parrish poster. The boy and his family pour out of the Rileys for a picnic. Camera follows boy as he climbs up on stage and begins conducting. A military band suddenly appears playing Elgar's *Enigma Variations*.

4. Close-up of boy gazing up at clouds where loud buzzing is heard. The band stops playing. Camera pulls back to show biplane landing in field of ferns and butterflies. The pilot, whose face is hidden, beckons. The boy climbs into the plane, and they soar into the sky. Bird's-eye view of countryside, lakes, mountains, oceans, South Sea isles. The pilot plays a record on a gramophone, a song from *The Fleet's In*. When the pilot turns around, she is Dorothy Lamour who says to the boy, "I believe that if a fella loved a girl he'd kiss her in the middle of the Rose Bowl on New Year's Day."

5. Long shot of another biplane, a German fighter piloted by Conrad Veidt dressed as the Red Baron and Peter Lorre as Dr. Caligari. Lorre cackles and machine guns the boy's plane, which dives in flames. The boy bails out. Lamour's sarong gets caught in the cockpit, and she goes down with the plane, laughing. Screen goes red.

II. Title: YOUTH

6. Blackout. Air raid sirens. Amplified explosions. Montage of battle and death scenes from Second World War, accompanied by Wagnerian music and intercut with sequences from *Metropolis* and *Siegfried*. Brigitte Helm leads masses of workers. Siegfried kills the dragon. Leni Riefenstahl dances on the seashore. Cut to young Russell projecting movies in home garage: Felix the Cat, Snub Pollard, and Betty Boop. Loud explosions as German bombs fall outside. Betty Boop winks lasciviously and begins to strip. The projector explodes in flames. Fade out.

7. Fade in on aerial shot of Pacific convoy. Cut to full shot of Russell as young man in white tropical shorts on bridge of Merchant Navy ship. In background a naked man, the Captain, stands on his hands. "Russell, you must get some long socks," says the Captain in heavy Scottish brogue. "Thick ones." Cut to Russell in long white socks. The Captain, still standing on his head, says, "They're no better. You'd better get long trousers." "Why, sir?" asks Russell. The Captain answers, "Dancer's legs." The ship's crew stares at Russell's legs. Russell dives overboard.

8. Intercut black-and-white still photographs of bombed-out streets of Southampton with color motion shots of young Russell at home listening to Tchaikovsky Piano Concerto and dancing around house to Stravinsky's *The Rite of Spring*. Freeze frame of Russell in mid-leap down stairs. Voice of his mother: "Well, Ken, you've got to do *something*."

9. Long shot of Russell arriving with stack of classical records at huge RAF training camp. Close-up of camp loudspeaker playing Shostakovich. Medium shot of RAF officer shouting, "All right, smash everything!" Pull back to show Russell vigorously leading other conscripts in destruction of equipment on abandoned airfield, all moving in unison to Shostakovich. Dissolve to Russell demobbed, holding letter of reference. Close-up of letter which reads: "The bearer will make an excellent picture-framer."

Russell in the RAF

Russell as photographer

10. Ballet audition in large London auditorium where Russell in khaki shorts and white gym shoes is dancing to *Swan Lake*. Old Russian ballet master shouts at him, "Pirouette!" Russell pirouettes and falls over. "Entrechat!" He leaps up and flaps his feet. "Tour en l'air!" He spins and falls. "Allez! Jump!" Russell jumps four feet. Thunderous applause. Russell jumps higher and higher. He is joined on stage by Betty Grable in transparent raincoat, white bootees, with umbrella. As scenery appears from *Springtime in the Rockies* and rain starts to fall, they dance and sing, "Run Little Raindrop Run."

11. Slow fade-in on gray winter sun. Dissolve to exterior of Brontë house in Haworth, then to interior for close-up of Shirley Russell in Victorian clothes on couch playing Charlotte Brontë. Harpsichord music. Pull back to show Russell with still camera. Rapid sequence of shots showing Russell directing and photographing Shirley in various poses throughout the house, then moving outside to shoot her walking across tombs of Brontë sisters in churchyard and trudging across soggy moors. Extreme close-up of Shirley's face resembling Louise Brooks in *Pandora's Box*.

Shirley Russell portrays
Charlotte Brontë
in photo by Russell

12. Orange summer sun fills the screen. Dissolve to colorful post-card version of Southampton beachscape looking like a set from *The Boy Friend*. Swimmers in twenties tank suits splash in the sea. Full shot of Russell in white bell-bottom slacks, blue sport shirt with yellow sleeveless sweater and red bow-tie, and Shirley standing beside him wearing Art Deco print two-piece dress with sailor top, both singing, "I Could Be Happy With You." Long shot of the couple with chorus line of swimmers on top of wings of airplane, dancing the Riviera and singing, "Flying Down to Rio." Slow fade as plane flies into the sunset.

III. Title: MATURITY

13. Exterior of front entrance to Pinewood Studios. Cut to Russell's POV as he passes through gate in Rolls Royce. Elderly gate attendant bows and says, "Good morning, Mr. Russell." As he drives through studio lot, executives, secretaries, craftsmen, and photographers line the road, waving and smiling. The Rolls stops. Russell gets out, wearing a monocle and jodhpurs. Camera follows him inside studio building where an assistant hands him a megaphone and a whip. He passes briskly through a door marked "ABSOLUTELY NO ADMITTANCE! ORGY SE-QUENCE!" and enters a huge sound stage made to resemble a craggy mountainslope. The slope is covered with hundreds of naked actors and actresses who snap to attention when Russell appears. He nods to the camera crew and then, crack-ing his whip, roars through the megaphone, "Right! Action!" As the orgy begins, *The Rite of Spring* is heard full volume. Suddenly Russell cracks the whip and shouts, "Halt!" Everyone freezes. Russell strides up the slope, stepping across sweaty entangled performers, and slightly rearranges the position of a small rock. After carefully studying the placement of the rock, he strides back down the slope, cracks the whip, and bellows, "Action!" Closeup of Russell's gleaming monocle.

Dance of the Seven Veils

14. Interior of immense Medieval inquisition room with white-tiled walls ornamented with bizarre instruments of torture. Critics, clerics, and other men of learning in long black judges' robes perch on extremely high stools. Camera follows Russell as he enters the room in a wheelchair, carrying a newspaper. A critic in bishop's garb asks, "Tell us, Russell, what possesses you to be so controversial?" Russell leaps from the wheelchair, rolls up the newspaper and pops the critic on the forehead. A musical note sounds. He goes around hitting everybody's head, each sounding a different note. By striking their heads, he plays the tune "See Me Dance the Polka at the Penguin Polka Ball." Enraged, the inquisitors grab Russell and plunge him into a tub of boiling water. He swims happily about in the steaming tub, bathing himself, squirting water through his mouth, and splashing the inquisitors who howl in pain.

15. Exterior of Madame Tussaud's Wax Museum. Camera tracks by long line of patrons through museum entrance past wax effigies of Sir Winston Churchill, the Beatles, the Pinball Wizard, and other famous British figures, then goes down dark stairway into a miniature cinema where a statue of Shirley stands at the door, holding a flaming torch. Costumed like a Pope, Russell's image is enthroned in the center of the auditorium, surrounded by wax dummies of Tchaikovsky, Mahler, and Freud dressed as the Marx brothers and an assortment of critics in clown makeup staring at a screen onto which are projected all of Russell's films in endless loops. As Strauss' *Death and Transfiguration* is heard in quintophonic sound, Russell begins to radiate an intense white-hot light that melts the audience. With a deafening crash, the auditorium ceiling splits open, revealing a lush blue Cecil B. DeMille sky. Kong's hairy hand reaches down from the heavens. Russell and Shirley ascend into the sky, glowing and singing, "We'll All Go Riding on a Rainbow." Iris out.

THE EARLY FILMS:

PEEP SHOW AND AMELIA AND THE ANGEL

Gene D. Phillips

One evening while I was in London, Ken Russell invited me to his home to talk about his early days as a filmmaker. Initially Russell had not wanted to be a film director but a ballet dancer. He worked hard at realizing this ambition, dutifully going to class every day and practicing in his London garret. "But I never became a good dancer," Russell concedes. "After working as a chorus boy in *Annie Get Your Gun*, as a mime in a terribly tatty touring company, and as an actor in another company that went bankrupt in three weeks, I gave up the stage — or rather the stage gave me up."

At this time, Russell read H. S. Ede's *Savage Messiah*, the biography of the struggling young sculptor Henri Gaudier, who became the subject of Russell's 1972 film. "This story about someone around my age at the time," he says "totally down and out but struggling onward nevertheless, gave me the courage to keep going, if not as a dancer then in some other art form. I was impressed by Gaudier's conviction that somehow or other there was a spark in the core of him that was personal to him, which was worth turning into something that could be appreciated by others. I wanted to find that spark in myself and exploit it for that reason."

*Russell's second film **Amelia and the Angel***

Russell decided to take up photography because he felt that it could lead to filmmaking. "At twenty-six I must have been the oldest student in London learning the basics of photography," he recalls. "I became fairly accomplished at it by photographing Shirley, whom I met at that time."

"I was studying fashion design," adds his wife Shirley Russell, "and we were hoping to get some pictures into *Vogue*, but the fashions I designed were thought to be too far out for those days."

Russell says, "I was not a magazine editor's idea of what a fashion photographer should look like. It wasn't fashionable in the 1950s for a fashion photographer to wear a bright sport shirt and denim trousers. You were expected to wear a Bond Street suit with a white carnation in the lapel. I couldn't even afford the carnation." Together they did photographic essays, which helped finance several amateur short films that enabled Russell eventually to get a job with BBC Television.

Russell's first film was called *Peep Show*. It is significant that, since so much of his later work would deal with the struggles of the artist, this beginning film would be about two kinds of purveyors of illusion. The first type is a group of con men who pose as disabled veterans to beg on the streets of London; the other are genuine performers, a pair of strolling players who do a pantomime routine in the street.

Because the film was made on an almost non-existent budget, Russell made a virtue of necessity by designing the picture in the style of a primitive silent film. The movie was shot silently, and a piano score was added to give the flavor of the nickelodeons. The dialogue titles, moreover, are chalked on sidewalks and fences.

Peep Show opens with the graduation ceremonies of the Bogus Beggars' Academy where the surly-looking "headmaster" is putting his latest batch of graduates through their paces to ensure that they are ready to take to the streets. He says, "I'll teach you how to limp properly," and then kicks one in the shins. Meanwhile, three alumni who are busy practicing their trade on a London sidewalk, discover that their business is falling off because pedestrians throw their spare change over a fence at something transpiring on the other side. The boss comes to look into the matter and, because neither he nor his men can find a spare knothole to look through, all four leap over the fence.

They find a father and daughter team doing a pantomime routine: the old man enacts the master of a life-size doll and the daughter (Shirley Russell) plays the mechanical doll. The old man takes the doll out of a huge box and winds it up. The doll begins to play a drum while he joins in with his clarinet. Their act ends with the doll locking its master into the box and collapsing, completely unwound.

The four men carry off the box, release the old man and force him to hand over all the coins. One of the group balks at his cohorts' mistreatment of the elderly gentleman, and the rest respond by knocking him cold and making off once more with the old man. The old man's daughter, who has witnessed these events, revives the reformed con man, and they pursue the others. But the girl's father, it turns out, can take care of himself: like a Pied Piper, he lures the four crooks with his clarinet tune into a river where they float off in the doll box they have been forced to convert into a raft.

Father and daughter are reunited and, together with the converted beggar, they dance off — not into the sunset but into the mist of a typically foggy London day. The crucial character, then, is the young man who begins by utilizing the art of illusion in his dishonest masquerade as a blind beggar and ends by joining the genuine practitioners of the art of illusion seeking to lighten the lives of others with their entertaining pantomimes. One is reminded of Luis Buñuel's remark that "the cinema is a dangerous and wonderful instrument if a free spirit uses it," dangerous only if used irresponsibly. "There are always some men who will try to express their inner world, to convey it to others through the medium of the film, which is above all a marvelous tool for artistic creation." There is no doubt that from the time of his first movie Ken Russell wanted to take his place among those free spirits, symbolized at the end of *Peep Show* by the exuberant trio that disappears over the horizon.

The second of Russell's amateur films was *Amelia and the Angel* which, according to him, was influenced by his conversion about that time to Roman Catholicism. "When I was young I really didn't know where I was going," he comments, "but as soon as I came into the faith my work, my philosophy, gained direction. Except for *The Boy Friend*, my films have been Catholic in outlook: films about love, faith, sin, guilt, forgiveness, and redemption — films that could only have been made by a Catholic." Significantly, all of these themes can be found implicitly in *Amelia and the Angel*, the most seminal of all of Russell's early works.

Both Ken and Shirley Russell were converted to Catholicism in 1957, and shortly afterward they decided to make a short film that would be a kind of religious valentine — indeed, the credits of the movie are enshrined in a lacey border that resembles a greeting card. Russell visited the Catholic Film Office in London, which at the time provided an information service on current films for Catholic subscribers. In addition, because the office occasionally produced and distributed short documentaries, Russell inquired whether or not they would like to back his film.

As it turned out, the office was primarily interested in producing documentaries that were mainly informational and so decided not to help produce the movie. One of the young priests associated with the office, however, was enthusiastic about Russell's project and offered to work on the script and help out in whatever way he could. As always, Shirley Russell provided the costumes and set about touring bargain basements and thrift shops to find material that she could transform into cheaply made costumes that would not look cheaply made, an ability which she has perfected over the years.

To play the key role of Amelia, Russell enlisted nine-year-old Mercedes Quadros, the daughter of the Ambassador from Uruguay to England at the time. Mercedes consented to play the part provided that Russell was willing to take her on an auto tour of London at breakneck speed. "She loved the ride," Russell remembers, "and all the while I was wondering if we would be arrested or killed before the day was over. Apart from that one rather bizarre request, however, Mercedes was very accommodating while we were shooting the picture. I got a letter from her and she said that making that movie was one of the most memorable experiences of her life. I still wonder if it is that ride round the city rather than appearing in the film that she remembers best."

Amelia and the Angel opens with a close-up of a curious machine that, in fact, was the forerunner of the modern phonograph and which played perforated metal discs. The sound track of the movie is made up of classical themes played on just such a machine. The camera pans from the ancient gramophone to a group of little girls dressed in angelic attire circling round a large rehearsal hall under the direction of their middle-aged teacher, Miss May. "Five girls in a play," the narrator intones, "and this is the story of Amelia, the least angelic of them all." The girls depart after their rehearsal concludes, and for a moment the large room is empty. Then the door at the far end of the hall opens cautiously, and Amelia reappears. Stealthily she snatches her pair of wings, of which she is particularly proud, and disappears out the door.

"She knew it was wrong," the narrator whispers confidentially, "but there she was taking the wings home to show her mother, even though Miss May had warned the girls that if anything happened to their wings they would not find another pair this side of heaven." Amelia rides home on the subway, and as she gets off the train, scrambles through the crowd of adults on the platform, protecting her precious wings. Russell photographs this scene from a low angle, showing how the world looks from the waist-high point of view of a child, allowing his handheld camera to be jostled in the same way that Amelia is.

Her jealous little brother makes off with the wings and frolics with them in a nearby park. As might be expected, he returns home with them torn and tattered, and Amelia is inconsolable. Through her tears she studies two religious pictures on her bedroom wall: one is an angel and the other a saintly artist holding a palette. She breathes a silent prayer and then runs out of the house and down the street, hoping that somewhere this side of heaven she can beg, borrow, or buy with the little money that she has a new pair of wings. The camera tracks laterally beside her as she runs from stall to stall in a sidewalk market nearly frantic with fear that she will not be able to appear in the school play.

Finally, Amelia spies a young woman carrying a pair of angel wings into a tenement. The little girl timidly walks up the stone steps to the porch. The camera shifts to inside the house as Amelia pushes the door open, giving the effect of an iris-in which reveals the child framed in the doorway. As she climbs the shadowy steps to the dark at the top of the stairs in silhouette, the scene takes on an unearthly, otherworldly atmosphere.

She goes into a room bathed in light where the young woman, now dressed as an angel, is posing for an artist. The pair are the embodiment of the two holy pictures which Amelia had prayed before back in her room at home. Both look down benignly at Amelia as she explains her plight. Without a word the painter climbs up an endless ladder out of the frame and after a moment climbs back down into view carrying a pair of angel wings for Amelia. (Just how high we are to infer that he had to soar in order to secure the extra wings for Amelia is a question that Russell prefers not to answer — in order to leave such speculations about the meaning of his little allegory to the moviegoer.)

Amelia laughs exultingly as she runs out of the building and disappears in the distance, holding the wings high above her head, and the film ends. The girl has experienced guilt and sorrow for disobeying Miss May, and as a result she has received a kind of symbolic absolution which is concretized in the granting of her prayer that she find another pair of wings. Here for the first time Russell deals with sin, guilt, forgiveness, and redemption, themes which will become much more apparent in his mature work.

Because of the promise which Russell demonstrated in his early amateur films, BBC-TV hired him in 1959 to work on a program called *Monitor*. "We made films on living artists and when there were no more of them left we turned to making films about dead artists," says Russell. "At first we were only allowed to use photographs and stills of these subjects but eventually we sneaked in the odd hand playing the piano and the odd back walking through a door. By the time a decade had gone by, these little boring factual representations of the artists had evolved into evocative films of an hour or more using real actors to impersonate the historical characters that we were portraying. We were encouraged by Huw Wheldon, who supervised the program. From that nucleus came John Schlesinger and some other film directors. In fact, *Monitor* was really the only British experimental film school."

Russell came to the BBC firm in the conviction he had learned from the short life of Henri Gaudier, "that everyone is a potential artist who has something in him which he can transmit to his fellows and which might well be of use to them. It is a pity when one, either through force of circumstance or because one is afraid of being ridiculed by others, won't produce and expose to everyone that little spark of something special which is unique to him alone. This is what I tried to do in my first steps in filmmaking in movies like *Amelia* and *Peep Show*."

That Ken Russell succeeded in doing just that is evidenced by the fact that his early short films, immature though they may be, are as unmistakably and uniquely his work as any film that he was to make in the years to come.

THE TELEVISION FILMS:

POET'S LONDON TO DANCE OF THE SEVEN VEILS

John Baxter

British critics, perennially derisive of the British Broadcasting Corporation, the authority which controls two-thirds of the material telecast in Britain and the bulk of its radio, have dubbed it "Auntie BBC." Yet while the Corporation has a well-deserved reputation for middle-class good taste, often at the expense of its more adventurous artists, it has also served the traditional valuable functions of aunts everywhere: helped nephews with their education, offered assistance in thin times and listened sympathetically to their complaints.

Ken Russell is only one of many directors who had their early training in British TV and returned to it often. Others include John Schlesinger, Jack Gold, Ken Loach, Jonathan Miller, Michael Apted and Claude Whatham. Russell is quick to acknowledge, though with reservations, its importance to his career: "Television, and particularly the BBC, is fine when you're starting out, as a film school and a place where one can try out one's ideas under fairly intelligent supervision; (and) on the whole I like the people in TV more than those in features."

On location for **Elgar**

Russell entered the BBC in 1959, given a job in the arts program *Monitor* on the basis of his amateur films, particularly *Amelia* and the Angel, a fantasy reflecting his strong interest at the time in Roman Catholicism. Between his first TV film, a 10-minute piece on the poet John Betjeman called *Poet's London*, broadcast in March, 1959, and February, 1970, when his controversial *Dance of the Seven Veils*, a violent debunking of Richard Strauss, had its sole TV airing, leading to mass protests and questions in Parliament, he made a further thirty-two films, a larger and more varied body of work than even his features.

Most of the films were 10 or 15-minute segments on the arts for *Monitor*, although when the program ceased production in June, 1965, he switched to the *Omnibus* series for his feature-length documentaries. *Monitor* producer Huw Wheldon, now head of BBC-TV, demanded of his directors — who included John Schlesinger, Jonathan Miller and Melvyn Bragg in addition to Russell — a respect for truth in reflecting the art scene of the day, but understood their wish to experiment with new techniques and approaches. Wheldon, however, rejected as "chi chi" Russell's attempt in *Poet's London* to film an incident from Betjeman's childhood in Edwardian dress, presaging his later interest in using costume and authentic locations to heighten biographical reality.

Most of Russell's films dealt with personalities then active in British literature, music and dance, all of whom he chose to film on location in landscapes which had a special significance to them and, on occasion, to the director. Writer Shelagh Delaney was taken back to her birthplace in the industrial North for *Shelagh Delaney's Salford* (September, 1960), and composer Gordon Jacob filmed in his cottage in the New Forest, an area which Russell loves and where he now owns a house. (*Gordon Jacob*, broadcast in March, 1959, also has an early example of close cutting to music, with Jacob's "New Forest Suite" set to pigs stampeding through the forest in search of acorns.)

Russell became *Monitor*'s expert in the eccentric. Although he did acceptable programs on choreographers Marie Rambert and John Cranko (January and April, 1960, respectively), films suggested by his previous unsuccessful career as a ballet dancer, his main interest was in bizarre independents and institutions on the fringe of the avant garde. *Portrait of a Goon* (December, 1959) examined the comic Spike Milligan, and *Pop Goes the Easel* (March, 1962) was a 40-minute study of four pop artists in which Russell personally demolished a piano with an axe as an example of action art. Both emphasized the grotesque and unconventional aspects of their subjects, often slightly at their expense.

21 /

Russell's affectionately mocking approach is apparent in his description of shooting *Old Battersea House* (June, 1961), a short film on a London suburban museum of pre-Raphaelite painting, particularly that of Evelyn de Morgan. "Mrs. Stirling, who was her sister, lived there and showed people over the house," states Russell, "She was ninety-nine then, dripping with white furs and jewels, and wearing an enormous hat. She could only walk with the help of two sticks and the place was so dark a servant followed her around with a lamp, and illuminated the pictures. Mrs. Stirling had a guided tour all memorized. 'My sister was at work on this painting of Azrael the Angel of Death when a frog hopped in and looked at it and hopped out again. £400 worth of lapis lazuli on that picture. Now over here . . .' and we went on through these huge rooms. People are always saying my films are bizarre but they pale beside reality."

Aside from one experiment in live TV, *Lotte Lenya Sings Kurt Weill* (September, 1962) on which co-director Humphrey Burton handled actual studio direction, Russell was, as Wheldon remarked, "very anxious to remain concentrated on film, an absolute specialist." Even the briefest of his *Monitor* films show a feature imagination, with lavish efforts often made to achieve a perfection few viewers appreciated. "He would go through a stone wall to get the right location" said Wheldon. "If it's necessary to be on the 54th floor then you go to the 54th floor and *certainly* you walk up the stairs."

Lonely Shore (January, 1964) illustrates Russell's insistence on authentic backgrounds. Based on the work of archaeologist Jacquetta Hawks, it was suggested by Wheldon who, Russell recalled, "had the idea of taking a look at our appliances and accouterments as they might appear to someone from another planet who was digging them up." In the film, aliens deduce — erroneously — many details of modern life from debris found half-buried in a sand bank. "We assembled a vast array of plastic tomato ketchup containers, club armchairs, cars, grand pianos, refrigerators, statues, staircases, fireplaces with dogs, etc." The objects were taken to Camber Sands, a bleak area in the Thames estuary, the only location which seemed to Russell to have the necessary lifelessness.

*Filming of mannequins for **The Lonely Shore***

"The day we shot this was the coldest, windiest day I've ever known. We had to wear goggles, the sand was so bad. I remember nailing a plastic bucket into the sand to stop it blowing away."

Elgar, first broadcast in November, 1962, and repeated at least three times, was both the culmination of Russell's early career and the beginning of his national reputation. As a celebration of the 100th *Monitor*, Wheldon wanted an entire 50-minute program de-

Filming of **Elgar**

Elgar

voted to one film, and chose Russell to make it. The British composer Edward Elgar had always interested Russell; both were Catholics, the sons of shopkeepers and had a reverent attitude to British landscape. He respected the fact that Elgar had "bettered himself," becoming famous with little formal training, as had Russell. It also provided a chance to pillory the British critics who had attacked Elgar's work; Russell had already experienced their anger over his use of the dramatized documentary style in *Prokofiev, Portrait of a Soviet Composer* (June, 1961) where, in a radical departure for the BBC and documentary in general, Prokofiev's life had been shown with the help of actors — admittedly photographed out of focus, reflected in a pond ("It must be a *murky* pond," the controller had allegedly demanded) or represented as a pair of piano playing hands.

Given approval for the Elgar project, Russell said immediately, "I can't do this without actors," and Wheldon agreed. A number of actors, mostly amateurs depersonalized in mid-shot, played the composer; and the film's romantic use of Elgar's music to underline his rise and disillusioned later years made it a hit. Its popularity earned Russell an invitation to direct *French Dressing*, but the feature's commercial failure and the lack of interest shown by producers in his idea to film the life of Claude Debussy drove him back to the BBC, for whom he made *The Debussy Film* in May, 1965.

Long kept out of circulation by legal objections from those associated with the composer's family, this documentary is one of Russell's most arresting works, exploring the relation between an artist and his associates, both professional and personal. Oliver Reed plays an actor about to star in a film on Debussy which Vladek Sheybal is to direct; they also play Debussy and his mentor Pierre Louys in the film-within-a-film of the composer's life. Russell praised the insight of Oliver Reed, still at that time a minor actor. "Oliver may not intellectually grasp an argument, or he may be exactly opposed to it, but sensually (he) can absorb some indefinable thing which is really the essence of the subject."

The Russell "stock company" of actors and technicians was already growing up around the director. Reed and Sheybal were

Oliver Reed in **The Debussy Film**

Russell with cast of **Diary of a Nobody**

Vivien Pickles,
Brian Murphy, and
Avril Elgar in
Diary of a Nobody

Murray Melvin in
Diary of a Nobody

*Georges Delerue during rehearsal for **Don't Shoot the Composer***

in many of his later films. So was Murray Melvin, who appeared in *Diary of a Nobody*, Russell's dramatization of the comic adventures of a twenties suburban family. Dick Bush, his BBC cameraman, was also to shoot *Savage Messiah* and Melvyn Bragg, his colleague on *Monitor*, to write others. With his relations with the cinema, particularly after the failure of *Billion Dollar Brain*, remaining strained, Russell concentrated on further BBC films, creating the four feature-length documentaries which many critics regard as his best work; *Isadora Duncan, The Biggest Dancer in the World* (September, 1966), *Dante's Inferno* (December, 1967), *Song of Summer* (September, 1968) and *Dance of the Seven Veils*.

Vivien Pickles in **Isadora Duncan, The Biggest Dancer in the World**

Russell directing **Dante's Inferno**

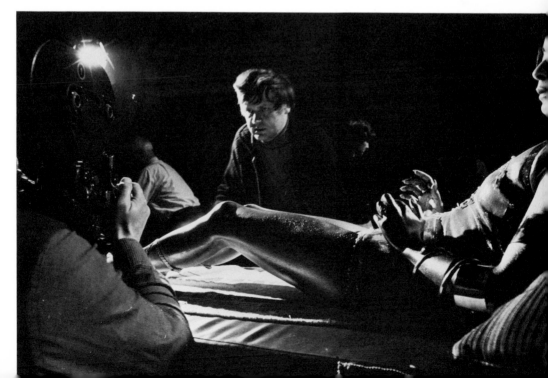

Russell conducting while Strauss makes loves in
Dance of the Seven Veils

Dance of the Seven Veils with Christopher Gable

Each of these films deserves more detailed consideration than is possible here. Their variety of style and approach reflects Russell's wildly vacillating personality, the films taking on the coloration of the moment. His picture of dancer Isadora Duncan is factually vague — the Hakim Brothers' ownership of most Duncan texts made it necessary to invent many incidents; the film's best scene, where Paris Singer presents his lover with a gift of six lady harpists, was pure fabrication but suggested by a true incident in

Ken Colley as Hitler
*in **Dance of the***
Seven Veils

*Reed and Judith Paris in **Dante's Inferno***

which he arranged for a full orchestra to greet her arrival on an apparently uninhabited island — yet it catches her extravagance and contempt for authority, while Oliver Reed's vision of the pre-Raphaelite poet and painter Dante Gabriel Rossetti is that of a man tortured by his remorse at the maltreatment of lovers and friends, and by the failure of his life to equal a vaulting imagination.

Meticulous as ever in his settings, Russell extended his care to the actors, all of whom, with the exception of Reed, were chosen for their physical resemblance to the pre-Raphaelite Brotherhood; they included painter Derek Boshier, poet Christopher Logue and a beautiful amateur named Gala Mitchell whose appearance as Jane, wife of William Morris, is one of hallucinatingly passive beauty.

Gala Mitchell in **Dante's Inferno**

Song of Summer, Russell's portrait of composer Frederick Delius in the last years of his life, remains the most popular of all his TV work, exceeding in appeal even *Women In Love*, a product of the same creative surge. Max Adrian's portrayal of the syphilitic Delius — the revelation of his fatal disease, hitherto kept secret, caused a mild stir — and Christopher Gable as his amanuensis Eric Fenby are vivid characterizations without losing focus; and the elegaic Delius music is aptly complemented by some of Dick Bush's richest images. As an affirmation of Russell's personal brand of Catholicism, with its emphasis on the cathartic value of sacrifice and the search for transcendence, the film has an even more vital relationship to later films like *The Devils*; but British TV audiences largely lost this underlying philosophical argument in their admiration of the film's tragedy and visual elegance.

Strauss plays for Goebbels, Hitler, and Goering in
Dance of the Seven Veils

The warmth of *Song of Summer* for its cantankerous subject left audiences unprepared for Russell's abrupt change of direction with his last BBC film, made eighteen months later when his attitudes had changed radically. All his bitterness was poured out on Richard Strauss, whom he represents as a character in a comic strip acting out distorted incidents from his operas and autobiographical symphonies. Long irritated with the romantic haze that had fallen over dramatized TV documentary since his defection to the cinema, and angered by "this awful civil service or academic way of doing films," Russell chose to attack the notion that "you could just dress people up in old clothes and it would suddenly be 'real.' I wanted to dress people up in clothes and do it in a totally *un*real way, but make it more real than ever." Such abrupt attacks serve to emphasize Russell's discomfort at working within the loose but nevertheless restrictive BBC structure.

35 /

Song of Summer with Max Adrian and Elizabeth Ercy

Adrian, Christopher Gable,
and Maureen Pryor in
Song of Summer

/ 36

Despite his frequent promises to return to TV, most recently with a project to film the life of Ralph Vaughan Williams, one wonders if this talented artist could now as readily adjust as he did in the sixties to a medium which, in return for its mass audience, demands that its artists pay at least lip service to contemporary standards. "The thing about the BBC," Russell remarks, "is that the quickness of the hand deceives the eye; before anyone can complain, the film is out. But the price you pay is that it's only shown once. If I could feel that films I did for TV were shown all over the world and were shown several times I'd probably never make another so-called 'feature film' again." But it seems doubtful that the BBC will ever be as quick again to place in Russell's hands so powerful a medium without satisfying itself that he would not turn it mercilessly on the society to whom it looks for support.

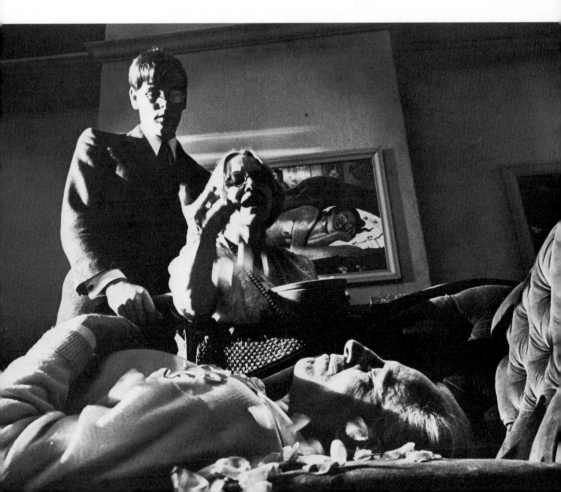

THREE MASTERPIECES OF SEXUALITY:

WOMEN IN LOVE, THE MUSIC LOVERS, AND THE DEVILS

Jack Fisher

The criticism of Ken Russell's films is very similar to the early criticism of D. H. Lawrence's novels. The words "obscene," "vulgar," "overwrought," "gaudy," "filthy," "trashy," appear with frenetic regularity in considerations of both artists. The association is apt, because Russell is attempting in his films the same deep probing of the emotions, particularly of the sexual emotions, that Lawrence examined in his novels. Their medium is different, but their message is much the same.

This is true not only of the Lawrence-Russell collaboration, *Women in Love,* but also of the other films I shall discuss here: *The Music Lovers* and *The Devils.*

At the core of each of these films, regardless of what they seem to be about, is an examination of some variety of sexual experience, in the unique Russell manner. Whereas Lawrence's forte was his ability to turn emotion into action, and by the action to discover some of the outlines of the emotion, Russell turns emotion into moving paintings. By means of movement, mass, color, and rhythm, he creates the visual equivalent of some aspect of sexual involvement.

Because his films seem to be about things other than what they are actually about — with the exception of *Women in Love* — there is considerable confusion about Russell's work. The critics, confronted with a work which doesn't stimulate what they are prepared to say, flounder and react negatively. The purpose of the following remarks is to attempt a reevaluation of the films in their own terms, with the hope of dissipating some of the confusion.

I. WOMEN IN LOVE

Women in Love is the most homogeneous of the three films. It seems to be about sexual relationships, and it is. It is also the film of Russell's which received the best press. This press coverage should have been more instructive, however, of Russell's methods than it was. To isolate these methods involves a review of the function of a movie director.

Russell directing Alan Bates and Eleanor Bron in **Women in Love**

Jennie Linden and Bates

Primarily, a director, in collaboration with his art department and his cameraman, decides how a picture will look. He establishes the physical context and photographic milieu that will provide clues to the film's intention. The physical and photographic world to a very large extent determines the emotional bias of the film.

Furthermore, the director, with his film editor, determines how a film will feel. By means of cutting and editing, the rhythm is established; rhythms which can vary from the soft elegiac flow of a Renoir, to the abrupt, percussive beat of a Guervas.

Glenda Jackson in Gudrun's dance with the cattle

In *Women in Love* there are two artistic consciousnesses at work: the vision of Lawrence which provides most of the words and actions, and Russell's which provides the shape, size, color, and rhythm — the visual attitude.

The director's visual attitude is as personal as his signature. With Russell the attitude inclines towards very pronounced forms: a remarkable range of colors from pastels to primaries and an increasingly restless rhythm in editing. There is also about his films a fascination with the decayed, the used, the soiled, the defective, and eventually with the grotesque. One of the problems with *The Boy Friend* is that the film is not substantial enough to support the innuendoes of the presentation. There is a definite von Stroheim style vision at work, a delight with the seedy, but the events

Bates, Bron, and Oliver Reed

are too trivial to be deepened by it. Russell needs full-blooded characters like Birkin and Gudrun, rather than Barbie and Ken, to support his mordant view of emotional connections.

Women in Love has a definite dated look about it, but it is more than dated. There is a tacky period feeling about the interiors, that comments upon the characters confined by the interiors. The feeling is intensified by Russell's extraordinary use of color. Ranging from the dark, suffocating browns, through red-golds, through the lush warm exteriors, to the green-white of the snow, the colors constantly reaffirm Russell's visual attitude toward events.

The scenes with Birkin and Ursula in the fields, for example, are full of warm, high value colors. The lighting is high key, and the overall high level of illumination helps to convey a total impression of opulent health and beauty. The sexuality is natural and satisfying. This mood is directly reinforced by the cross-cutting to the drowned couple who are in exactly the same position as Birkin and Ursula, but frozen in an atmosphere of stillness, with the colors changed to grays and greens, the amount of white down, and the overall lighting low.

Contrasting these two parallel scenes, one begins to sense Russell's aim. By a rigid control of the surrounding atmosphere, he presents us with the nature of the sexual experience being observed. Birkin and Ursula come together in a context which is natural, healthy and frantic. The screen is full of light; the editing quick and pulsing. It is one of the most erotic scenes on film, partly because the sensuality is so open, primitive, and free. Russell manages the *mise en scene* with great control. The result is that sex is sex, not the super romantic Elvira Madigan sex, but in its own way just as beautiful. The scene of the drowned couple is, on the other hand, a visual statement of the destructive potentials of possessiveness.

The scene of Critch's seduction of Gudrun is a further and different statement of sexual relationship which bears a clear visual attitude. There is no light. The room is crowded and dingy. The actions are furtive. Interestingly enough, the editing manages to

convey a frantic quality but not the impulsiveness of Birkin and Ursula. Instead the atmosphere is brutal, close to rape.

In David Lean's *Ryan's Daughter* there are two sex scenes which very nearly parallel scenes in *Women in Love*. The attitude and effects are different. In the bedroom where Russell sees brutality, Lean settles for mechanics. In the exteriors both directors present erotic fulfillment, but Lean's is more lyrical, less impulsive.

The most famous scene in both the book and film of *Women in Love* is the nude wrestling match between Birkin and Kritch. It is clearly a scene involving sex, if not actually an overt sex scene. Russell manages the elements to create a mood of healthy sexual vitality which intensifies the normal relationship between the men. Kritch is open and comfortable, Birkin becomes so as the scene progresses. The atmosphere affects them. The size of the room, the modulations of red-gold, and the vitality of the action, plus extremely mobile camerawork remind us of the field scene in spite of the locale being an interior. Russell is, by and large, not too kind to homosexuality in his films. But in this scene he conveys an attitude which is positive: a faithful rendering of the masculine athletic brutality, and the tender undercurrent of a healthy relationship. Perhaps his objection is only to effete homosexuality.

This is a good example of the way Russell treats his material. The action itself in the scenes is important. Russell records this well. He also visualizes the resonances of the action in an attempt to transmit directly the nature of the experience, through purely sensual imagery.

If one watches Russell's films with open eyes, and with a mind open to experience, the sensual assault of his films is not only stimulating emotionally but intellectually as well. It must be understood, however, that the conceptual suggestions produced are more related to paintings than to plays. Plays appeal through the ear to the mind in the socially conditioned medium of words. Paintings appeal through the eyes in the unsocial media of color, shape and line. Plays produce concepts which are more "literary"; the concepts can be easily verbalized and intellectualized. Paintings produce ideas which are non-verbal and related to harmonies of the intellect rather than to the arguments.

Van Gogh, Monet, or Renoir produce such intellectual suggestions by their paintings. Russell is related to them and to understand and appreciate his work, one must appreciate the suggestiveness of his work rather than the argumentation. Because he is a motion picture director, his use of the medium as a means of motion painting involves certain restrictions. The nature of the medium, including its use of people, inclines towards representational art. If the director's inclination is towards abstraction, toward essential rather than accidental statement, then the problem becomes one of manipulating the representational to produce the abstract, a problem somewhat similar to surrealism with the added difficulty of maintaining a narrative line.

Perhaps it is because he is dealing with Lawrence in *Women in Love*, and because Lawrence too is concerned with creating visibility for the abstract, that Russell is somewhat constrained in the film. This may not be apparent at the time, but after seeing the next two films it is clear that *Women in Love* is only incipient Russell, whereas *The Music Lovers* and *The Devils* are Russell in the grand manner.

II. THE MUSIC LOVERS

The Music Lovers is one of the best, yet most universally-damned, of Russell's films. Because the film involves Tchaikovsky, and despite the title which clearly announces a focus on the parasites around Tchaikovsky, everyone expected the film to be another Cornel Wilde-Chopin, Robert Walker-Brahms type of movie. Although it clearly wasn't from the first scenes, the power of fixation is so great that critics refused to accept the obvious. No one was ready to accept it as a new kind of biography: a biography of the crippling forces including the crippling malaise of homosexuality in the life of a talented man. So the film was categorized and condemned.

If one can forget categories like "musical biography" or even "biography" and look at the film as what it seems to be — a serious study of sexuality, with Tchaikovsky used as the focus of the study

Richard Chamberlain in **The Music Lovers**

— the effect of the totality is quite different from what the critics suggest. That the film is about sex seems beyond argument. In it is reviewed every kind of sexuality imaginable except "normal" heterosexuality and perhaps zoophilia. There are several varieties of homosexuality, at least two varieties of inverted heterosexuality, incest, sadomasochism, voyeurism and even a suggestion of displaced necrophilia. There is so much sex in the film that if it were all removed, what would remain would be a fifteen minute entertainment starring Max Adrian.

Glenda Jackson and Chamberlain

Granting, then, that the film is only apparently a musical biography and is actually a study of sexual inter-relationships, the interesting question is: what does Russell see in these relationships, and how does he transmit his vision? To answer the question involves once again careful attention to decor, to color, to photography, and to editing — the director's proper tools.

The most efficient way to consider *The Music Lovers* and *The Devils* and with them Russell's methods is to look at the various grand tableaux around which the films are constructed. There is an increasingly large number of these set pieces in both of these films (and in Russell's *The Boy Friend*). Grand tableaux refers to those moments when the forward progress of the narrative is slowed and a segment brought into focus, which by its arrangement, color, shape, makes some kind of comment on the surround-

Tchaikovsky's marriage

ing action, and by its duration makes an important comment on the entire film.

In *The Music Lovers,* such a scene occurs early in the film: the flashback to Tchaikovsky's time in the country with his sister. The scene is idyllic, full of warm gold colors, graceful birches, and action that is slowed down to near floating buoyancy. The scene is a little reminiscent of Widerberg's *Elvira Madigan,* in that both are highly stylized in order to convey the rapture of love and unity with nature. Bo Widerberg creates the scene in order that the mood can blossom into fully expressed love.

In *The Music Lovers* the same potentials are involved, but since the love cannot develop the scene merely provides the exposition for Tchaikovsky's hangup about his sister. There is innocence and sensuality, but the sensuality is submerged and displaced. Without a word, and with only the sound of the piano concerto,

51 /

we are presented with the essentially childish nature of Tchaikovsky and the child-like character of his incestuous attraction. Since most psychiatry, especially Freudian, associates incest fears with homosexuality, this idyllic scene is not included just for its prettiness. The scene provides a visual set of facts for the major statement of the film: Tchaikovsky's homosexuality and the vulnerability which it creates in him to the people around him.

Homosexuality is certainly the most important factor in the railway carriage scene, where Russell deserts the impressionistic methods of the field scene and returns to the dark, low value colors of the interiors in *Women in Love*; the colors are of the heavy academy pictures of the 19th century. This color scheme

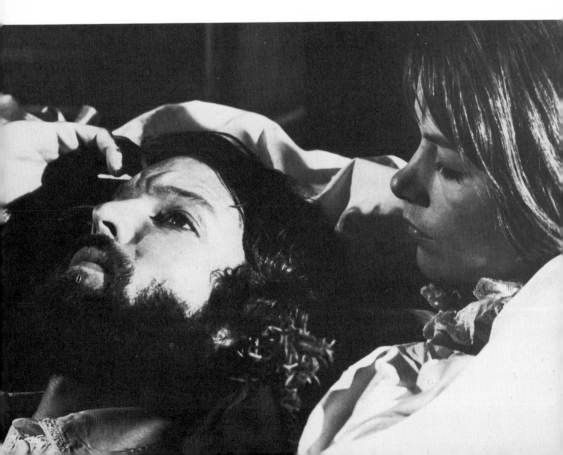

alone implies that the scene will be neither happy nor fulfilling, which in the context of the action means definite premonition.

But no warning can prepare us for what the scene offers, a direct transmission of the atavistic horror which a homosexual feels when confronted by an aroused woman. As arranged by Russell, the scene is not intended as a description of the confrontation but as an involvement in the actual dynamics of the situation. The camera work and the editing create a sense of growing terror. Building upon the original motion of the train and then developing an artificial motion which becomes psychologically descriptive, the rhythm of the scene builds as each character becomes more distraught. In the rising tension of the scene, the inhibitions of homosexuality become a metaphor of all of the dark forces which strain the relationships between men and women.

There have been homosexual scenes in other films, such as *Midnight Cowboy* and *Sunday, Bloody Sunday,* but to my knowledge none of them have attempted to translate the prime emotional factors into cinematography. If only for this one dazzling display of brilliance, *The Music Lovers* is worth seeing. There are other memorable scenes, however, all related to the burden of homosexuality.

The narrative-visual device of the death of Tchaikovsky's mother, for example, is extraordinary. In these sequences and flash-cuts, Russell indulges his taste for the macabre and grotesque, and simultaneously transmits to the audience a sense of the horror felt by the tormented composer. This is no member of Gay Lib we are watching but a person tortured by his conditioning past. When Tchaikovsky hears his mother's voice and rushes into the steaming bathroom, the atmosphere created suggests demonism. The milieu of the party, the dark colors and congested decor, the halls and stairs and doors, and the present-past intercuts produce the sensation of madness, a madness later built upon and reinforced in the railway scene.

None of these scenes, condemned though they were, received the scorn of the 1812 Overture fantasy. Certainly to anyone who is expecting José Iturbi to appear in this part of the movie and

Chamberlain and Christopher Gable

play "Tonight We Love," the fantasy scene must be a shocker. To anyone who has been paying attention to the sexual and visual structure of the film, however, the fantasy is a logical development of the abnormal.

Apart from the psychiatric content of the fantasy — the destruction of the "music lovers" with the surrogate penis of the cannon, which is not an inconsistent sex-wish for the patient we have been watching — the most interesting aspect of the scene is Russell's versatility in "painting" the scene. Suddenly both impressionist and academy colors and forms are gone, and the dream is presented in terms of the surrealistic. Within the scene there are hints of Miro, Tchelitchew, and Chagall.

There is a childish quality which is completely consistent with the child-man, trapped in incestuous fixation, unable to function as a mature man, except in music. I don't believe I have ever seen a montage arrangement describing success, the taking of the world by storm, that is any clearer and romantically satisfying than the end of the fantasy which then dissolves brilliantly to the leaden grey reality of the statue of Tchaikovsky in the midst of a colorless world. Within these few minutes we are shown what it is like to be swept up by fame, and then in the dissolve the frenzy dies down and becomes stale. All of this is clear and precise in painter's terms, and all is done without a single word.

It is impossible to leave *The Music Lovers* without mentioning the series of shots which end the film, the various views of the wife looking out of the asylum window. Suddenly all of the luxuriant color of the film is reduced to greys and greens. The frenzy of the asylum is frozen in geometric arrangements. Strip by strip, the surface world is peeled away, and we are left with a composition which suggests Mondrian out of Edvard Munch, and which produces an ultimate statement of alienation and desertion. The final tableau of the single eye fixed in the rigidity of the rectangular lines is one of the greatest single shots I have ever seen in a film. It is closely followed in effect by the final shot in *The Devils*.

III. THE DEVILS

However one regards the earlier films, it seems impossible that anyone can watch *The Devils* and not be aware of Russell's brilliance as a visual artist. The film is so totally visual that one has the feeling of watching a series of single frame paintings being displayed. It is therefore difficult to discuss *The Devils* in terms of a few scenes because so many are memorable; yet since the film is again about sex and sexual aberrations, perhaps it may be helpful to single out scenes illustrative of Russell's brilliant handling of the subject.

In the opening scene, for instance, we are confronted with what proves to be a transvestite performance. It is strange, exotic, and very sick. The decor and photography identify the situation as not only homosexual but of a peculiarly virulent variety. The destructive queen is to be feared under any circumstances, and

Georgina Hale and Oliver Reed in **The Devils**

woe to the day when the queen is a king. This scene alone, with
its echoes of the madness of Camus' Caligula, should alert anyone
watching that the film is about sexual inversion, its spread and
effect, from the King on down through the Kingdom in a kind of
pathological ratio. But critics saw only church and state in the film.

Vanessa Redgrave

Unlike the people in *The Music Lovers,* the priest Grandier is quite normal, and considering his calling, embarrassingly heterosexual. This single fact lends a balance to *The Devils* that was missing in the previous film. We have some norm by which to judge the abnormalities.

A norm is useful, because we must remember at all times that we are in an entirely alien land. It is a waste of effort for anyone to look to the real biographies of the people Russell recreates, or in the case of this film to Huxley, or Whiting, or Richelieu, or France at any time. The worlds which Russell manipulates may seem to be like others, but actually they are much closer to the paintings of Chagall and Klee than to any historical or scientific reality.

In the case of *The Devils*, the example of Grandier, the normality of his emotions and the sanity of his politics, work as a kind of guide through the sexual-visual wonderland, and produce a scene in the movie, which I found almost unbearably tender and beautiful — the scene of Grandier and his wife in bed. The total effect of the scene is like an exquisite Japanese print. The tone and rhythm are subdued, warm, and loving, the color and lighting low-value, low key. The composition is simple and completely uncluttered: two heads and shoulders on pillows. The scene is a visual key to the film, as well as an example of Russell's ability to visualize precisely an emotional mood. If we understand what is happening in the scene — honest lovemaking between two loving people — and if we then notice how this is surrounded visually, we have a good insight into the inner torment of the other scenes and their visual equivalents.

There are any number of examples of tormented visualization involving the Mother Superior in the convent — not the fantasies because they have an entirely different kind of visualization but the scenes of the solitary black forms, isolated and alone in the midst of shiny white tile rooms. Quite apart from the narrative line, the color and compositions within the convent (the humpbacked nun becoming a painter's asymmetrical mass in the surrounding grey and grey-white and white curves of the rooms) are so visually powerful that the film could be silent and still be effective. What more stunning visual metaphor for the psychological suffocation of the Mother Superior than to stuff her deformed body into the tiny lookout space from which she watches her fantasy lover? The mere confinement of mass in congested space creates an understanding of the annihilating pressures of her sexual drive.

In the convent scenes it should be obvious that Russell is experimenting extensively with white. With the various whites of the convent, the white of the city and the white of the city walls, he seems to be establishing a leitmotif of whiteness which resists and dissolves natural relationships. The use of white increases until it reaches an apotheosis at the end when the wife, Madeleine,

Gemma Jones and Redgrave

escapes the ruined city. Leaving behind her dead husband, she walks down a long road, while the color literally bleeds out of the film. The final scene is almost black-and-white with white and its virulent associations ascendent. In terms of pictorial qualities alone the ending is triumphant cinema.

The Devils is so totally and maniacally hated by nearly every critic I have read that it seems an exercise in excess to select the parts which are hated more than the entire film. The winners, I think, are the sequences involving the nun's lewd fantasies of performing fellatio on her priest-chevalier who has become Christ, and the sequences in which the nuns are exorcised by vaginal hydraulics. Naturally enough, the scenes have a great deal more to them than meets the eye.

59 /

Christopher Logue as Richelieu

The purging of Sister Jeanne

Michael Gothard as the professional exorcist Barré

The exorcism scenes are indeed raunchy, but the whole world of satanic and counter-satanic belief is raunchy. Devil worship usually centers on a whole series of perverted sexual acts. The church of the Middle Ages and the Renaissance was more pragmatic about these things than our modern sense of propriety wants to allow. The incidence of genital irrigation, usually with boiling water, is one aspect of Russell's film that *is* historically accurate, not that this fact matters to him or to anybody concerned with the reality of the film.

Georgina Hale as Phillipe with medieval witch doctors
played by Max Adrian and Brian Murphy

*The rape of Christ sequence which was cut from the film
at the request of the studio and censors*

What clearly does matter to Russell in the scenes are the possibility of conveying sexual and religious hysteria, and the cumulative effects of sexual repression. What Russell produces is visual demonism reminiscent of the asylum scenes in *The Music Lovers*. The scene is also reminiscent of Hieronymus Bosch, a painter who seems to interest Russell.

The single word which describes the scenes is chaos — but not in the artistic execution. There are occasions when we may feel that Russell merely enjoys swinging a camera around in the wildest gyrations, but in this scene the device is an apt one. The photography and editing are amazing. He manages to encompass a roomful of hysterical nuns, and by a series of close-up, long-shot, medium-shot combinations he captures the sense of individual torment in the midst of an inverted orgy. The total effect is a

63 /

combination of sensuality without eroticism, masochism in its ugliest stages, and a kind of communal madness that suggests the camps of the demonic Third Reich. Working always within the astringent white tile with the suggestive Romanesque lines, Russell amasses sound and pictures that produce a sterile, lustless impact which is exactly the opposite of arousal. He may disgust some people, but he does so in search of the accurate metaphor. He would not settle for Polanski's cheap, easy, cosmopolitan view of demonism in *Rosemary's Baby*.

The fantasy scenes present a different kind of problem. They have qualities which are erotic, and yet they are clearly the eroticism of a deranged consciousness. They are projected by a very sick lady in heat. Russell's solution is ingenious and successful. By the use of different film stock and filters, he creates a period fantasy in sepia colors, a Cecil B. DeMille religious pornie. The choice

Sister Jeanne's vision

is perfect because DeMille's films usually teetered on the edge of the obscene. The more religious his films were, the more they teetered. In his *King of Kings* he got more mileage out of Mary Magdalene than out of Jesus. And many people watched these films and confused the itches which were aroused with spiritual stirrings. Portraying the nun's fantasies in the style of Cecil B. DeMille is more than an accurate representation; it is expressing the exact quality of the lust hidden in ecclesiastical trappings and is thus precisely right for the Mother Superior.

Throughout all of these films — *Women in Love, The Music Lovers,* and *The Devils* — the ability to paint and visualize emotional moods stands out as the single most impressive aspect of Ken Russell's talent. Few directors today can compose the individual pictures, color them, and film them so that they take on a complete resonating structure of their own.

Russell follows the tradition of Flaherty and especially of Eisenstein in being a meticulous composer. Like the Soviet director he uses elaborate trappings not for their own sake but to provide the visual milieu which will comment on the action described. Russell's aim in painting motion pictures is precision and complexity of statement — the same as any painter's. In addition, by means of superb editing and fluid photography, Russell gives the paintings the extra dimension of rhythm.

Any discussion of Russell should mention his other skill as a director: an ability to elicit excellent performances. The Russell company of actors who appear more or less consistently in his films is an extremely talented group, and their performances for him are always in top form. Glenda Jackson, of course, has emerged as one of today's leading film actresses. Her performances for Russell are her best work because in his films she accomplishes acting tasks that are really difficult. Vanessa Redgrave, who is in danger of becoming the Katherine Cornell of the Revolution, gets down to business for Russell and also accomplishes difficult tasks. (After seeing Russell's brilliant *Isadora Duncan, the Biggest Dancer in the World,* with Vivien Pickles, one wishes he had directed Redgrave in her little Isadora Duncan pastiche.)

The execution of Grandier

Oliver Reed, graduated from earlier comedies, has developed into an actor of truly commanding power while working for Russell. Richard Chamberlain finally found in Russell a director who could free him from his MGM image; and Max Adrian, an accomplished performer appearing in virtually everything Russell has directed, was given a chance to display his versatility and to create at least one unqualifiedly brilliant performance as Delius.

This ability to create situations that encourage such fine performances in his actors is related to a consistency of attitude found in all of Russell's films — his respect for the natural and the free. Although critics often accuse him of overly emphasizing degenerate and degrading aspects of life, it should be remembered that he points up these aspects chiefly in connection with characters who are phony, sick and deranged. Other characters in his work, such as Grandier and his wife in *The Devils* and Birkin and Ursula in *Women in Love,* are developed with respect and dignity.

In my opinion Ken Russell is a genius, by which I mean that his films are extraordinary, unique, and provide a view of the world that is new and profound. Like D. H. Lawrence, whose view of life was similar, Russell must bear the calumnies of his contemporaries. But I believe that time, as it did with Lawrence, will permit even critical minds to expand.

Savage Messiah *with Scott Antony*

RUSSELL'S METHODS OF ADAPTATION:

SAVAGE MESSIAH AND TOMMY

Joseph A. Gomez

I. SAVAGE MESSIAH

It has always been much easier for critics to dismiss Ken Russell's work as "excessive" and "outrageous" than to do the homework necessary to understand the nature of the unique methods and personal vision of the filmmaker who depends almost entirely on adapting his films from other (usually literary) sources. In Russell's case, in fact, one cannot dismiss the consideration of transformations from literature to film as a useless pedantic exercise — especially since so many ill-informed critics seem to agree with Robert Hughes' claim that his major enterprise is the "disembowelment of history." Of course, Russell's films must stand on their own, but a study of his methods of adaptation provides valuable insights into his particular vision. For unlike many other filmmakers, such as Sidney Lumet, John Schlesinger, and Tony Richardson who also depend almost exclusively on literary sources, Russell clearly exhibits a unified style of adaptation.

Although he has made films from novels and plays, Russell is especially attracted to the genre of biography and most notably to the lives of artists in conflict with society. He developed his personal approach to the "bio-pic" during his ten years of making BBC films, and at the same time began his experiments with shock editing and unconventional use of music. Russell's richly ornate images, his craving for the theatrical, his ambivalent attitudes towards his heroes, and his bizarre sense of humor have disoriented and alienated many viewers, but he always finds some significant factual or aesthetic basis for even his most extravagant embellishments. If he frequently violates "the letter" by adding, subtracting, telescoping, and rearranging events, he captures "the spirit" or essence of his characters more convincingly than many so-called historically accurate translations.

Russell, however, is rarely content with just presenting the essence of his protagonists. His films are outstanding examples of the "kick 'em in the crotch" school of overstatement, but he also creates subtle aesthetic patterns and nuances frequently ignored by hostile reviewers. In an attempt to jolt people into awareness, he forces his audience by the often irritating manipulation of anachronisms to relate his heroes to the present day world. *The Devils* is not merely a supercharged historical recreation of the last years of Urbain Grandier; it is also an aesthetically exciting, visionary film about our own time.

Russell's "quiet, little film," *Savage Messiah*, serves as a good example of his methods and concerns. The film is far less complex than most of the other feature biographies; and its subject, the French sculptor Henri Gaudier-Brzeska who died at age twenty-four, is relatively obscure. In fact, there have been only three books written about him: H. S. Ede's *Savage Messiah*, Ezra Pound's *Gaudier-Brzeska: A Memoir*, and Horace Brodzky's *Henri Gaudier-Brzeska 1891-1915*.

Gaudier-Brzeska is a figure who has held a powerful personal attraction for Russell since he first encountered Ede's biography when he himself was a struggling young artist. Russell in this film uses the sculptor to embody many of his own views on the artist in society. Some of the concepts come directly from Ede's book, but many build from where the book stops. In some respects the film is an accurate portrait both of Henri Gaudier-Brzeska and Ken Russell.

The film depicts an unusual Platonic love affair, and the brief note ("the story of a young French artist and the Polish woman he

Antony and Dorothy Tutin

met just before World War I'') after the title reinforces this fact. Russell, like Ede, begins his portrait with this meeting because he sees the relationship with Sophie Brzeska as the necessary catalyst for his protagonist's creative activity. Early in the film Henri tells Sophie, ". . . sometimes I don't think that I'll be able to do what I want to do, on my own." The film's structure and dominant visual rhythms emphasize the uneasy Platonic union formed by two very different individuals as protection against the forces of a hostile world.

While Christopher Logue's script uses material from all three accounts of Henri's life, the film is primarily adapted from the Ede biography, which consists chiefly of Henri's letters interspersed

71   /

with the author's commentary. Ede provides essential information, avoids speculation and refrains from personal comment beyond that which is absolutely necessary. Logue and Russell in their portrait of the Gaudier-Brzeskas speculate widely, interpret freely, fill in gaps suggested by Ede's work, and treat some of their protagonists' fantasies as reality. The intensity, enthusiasm, and childlike exuberance of Henri, documented frequently both in Ede's and Brodzky's accounts, is appropriately complemented by Russell's flamboyant filmmaking style.

The opening of the film is a remarkably accurate visual representation of Ede's description of the meeting between Henri and Sophie at St. Genevieve Library in Paris. But Russell shapes his material more effectively than the rambling account by Ede. Immediately after the opening sequence, for instance, Russell creates a vignette which not only expresses the charm and energy of Gaudier, but also establishes the central motif of external rejection versus belief in the self.

While talking to Sophie (played by Dorothy Tutin) about his genius and his ability to create beauty, Henri (Scott Antony) leaps upon some conventional statues by a fountain and proclaims his views on art to the public: "Art is dirt. Art is sex, and art is *revolution.*" The police, of course, care nothing about art but much about public morality; and Gaudier is forced to flee. This fabricated episode then sets up a motif which will be repeated throughout the film. Although in conflict with each other (Sophie, who is writing a book entitled *Truth: a Novel of the Spirit,* claims that "art is *above* sex"), both battle together against the limitations and hostility of the outside world.

Russell's chief method for the delineation of Sophie's character in the early section of the film is a monologue of her past life. The language of the script at this point owes much to the second chapter of Ede's *Savage Messiah,* but again Russell uses the source material for his own purposes. The sequence goes beyond the mere revelation of Sophie's frustrations; it is an attempt to suggest something of Henri's drawing methods. Chopping vegetables, Sophie pours forth her life story at breakneck speed, while Henri listens from a chair and begins to sketch her. The audience, for the

most part, sees her from his viewpoint. The bust shots, the intense close-ups of her head and hands, the occasional re-establishing full shots of Henri, and the final glimpse of the drawing simulate the creation of a sketch.

The next sequence, however, owes little to fact, except that Henri had an interest in primitive art and visited the Louvre with Sophie shortly after their agreement to establish an "artistic companionship." As they walk to see Henri's "real" mother, the Louvre, the dialogue concerns Henri's ideas about the relationship of the present to the past in art, without attempting to deal with the complexities of the historical Henri's Bergsonian theories. The entire sequence, however, helps to establish the motif of rejection basic to the film. The improperly dressed Henri wanders through the rooms amid lifeless paintings viewed by lifeless people presented in "cut-out" fashion; and finally, pursued by museum guards, he climbs atop a huge stone head from Easter Island and lectures in flamboyant fashion to the staid onlookers enjoying the so-called benefits of cultural democracy. "Art is alive. Enjoy it. Laugh at it. Love it or hate it, but don't worship it. You're not in church." Henri and Sophie are forcibly ejected — right into the midst of a passing funeral procession. Then they decide to go to the country, but Henri's "natural" mother treats them little better.

Sophie's eviction from a cottage near the home of Gaudier's parents is a fact, and Russell's presentation parallels the Louvre episode and reinforces the rejection motif. Sophie's talk with Henri about her past loneliness and inability to kill herself because she was "afraid of the darkness and the worms" is taken directly from

Ede's account, and an actual anonymous letter accusing Sophie of "the improper reception of men" is also used by Russell. He sees Henri's mother as the culprit and stresses Henri's violent reaction to the accusation.

In London the couple reside at the Putney Arch studio, which the historical Henri only found in the last year of his life in London. Many of the short sequences of their early life there (Sophie begging with "her baby," a doll wrapped in a shawl; Henri translating letters for his Norwegian employer and visiting a five-bob whore but "doing nothing" except making a few sketches of her) were constructed from a factual base and reshaped by Russell to reinforce the dominant motifs of rejection and conflict which permeate the film.

If the Gaudier-Brzeskas stand in marked contrast to bourgeois conventionality, they are not the darlings of the bohemian world either. Ede's biography documents that Henri attended dinner parties similar to the one at Corky's: "A Russian actress — a woman

with a monocle and pretty stupid, asked in French to explain to her futurism and cubism. When for a joke I made her believe that it had to do with homosexuality, she asked me to go and see her on Thursday evening." Russell's caricatures of Corky's associates are extreme; he creates a glimmering gallery of malicious, decadent, pompous fools led by an epicene art dealer named Shaw, whose sole function seems to be "to depress art." The remainder of the group, except for Corky, is presented as poisonous poseurs who possess neither talent nor character when compared to the Gaudier-Brzeskas, the only three-dimensional individuals in the film and the sole characters with real names.

Aside from counterpointing Henri's values, Shaw sets up one of the film's key sequences by baiting Henri into making an offer to show him a non-existent statue. With assistance from Corky and Sophie, Gaudier steals a suitable piece of marble from a graveyard and in a frenzy creates "Torso" in a mere six hours.

Although obviously exaggerated, the event is based on Gaudier's life. Ezra Pound notes in his memoir of Gaudier that when passing a certain cemetery, Henri often marvelled at the waste of good stone, and Frank Harris tells the story that Gaudier created his first carvings when Jacob Epstein told him that he would come to see his work. "So Gaudier at once went out, got three small stone blocks, and by working more or less night and day had something ready by Sunday." The torso sequence, moreover, allows Russell to show that "artistic achievement is usually 5 percent inspiration and 95 percent perspiration and hard slog" and to present a context for Gaudier's monologue which reveals some of the artistic attitudes held in common by both Gaudier and Russell.

Henri philosophizes and chips away at the marble stone: as the rhythmic ticking of the chisel accompanies his voice, the constantly moving camera sweeps in the 180° angle, then slowly up, then down; and the audience begins to see the form take shape. The superb lighting and *mise-en-scene* allow the viewers to gain some sense of the texture of the stone itself. For Henri, each blow must be true, and because of that, "every blow is a risk." Yet for Henri art is not magical or mystical:

You can always tell a bad artist, like a bad doctor, by the fact that he tries to surround his words with some hocus-pocus. Sure there's a mystery, but there is as much a mystery to the one who is doing it as to the one who is looking at it ... But, by and large, it would be wrong to be taken in by that solitary genius stuff. Of course, I do it because it pleases me. There is nothing wrong with that. But if it don't give me a lot doing it, how the hell is it going to give anything to anybody else. That's the mystery, Porkums.

Russell's Henri Gaudier-Brzeska, however, is as much passion as perspiration. After Henri completes the torso in a single night, Shaw does not bother to keep his appointment; and Russell fabricates an incident in which Henri carts his newly created piece to Shaw's and then proceeds to throw it through the gallery window. The short, ironic scene showing Henri forcibly removed from a cell and the jailhouse, because Shaw has dropped the charges, is filmed in a fashion that parallels the expulsion from the Louvre. Yet another variation of this motif of battling hostile external forces occurs only a few scenes later when Henri and Gosh Boyle are thrown out of the Vortex, Shaw's anachronistically garish nightclub.

Gosh Boyle, the most outlandish female character in the film, is similar to Shaw; as he is used to counterpoint Henri, Gosh contrasts with Sophie — at all levels from social to sexual. Both women, for instance, sing ridiculous songs. The historical Sophie often sang her Polish folk melodies for guests, and Russell's Sophie sings about the lives of two fleas as a commentary on her own existence, as a half-insane cry from the depths. Gosh's plea of "Votes for Women," on the other hand, is merely a faddish attempt to save herself from boredom. Russell ruthlessly ridicules Gosh not because she is a feminist but because she is a shallow, spoiled fool who has silly illusions of grandeur. When descending a staircase nude and dancing à la Isadora Duncan, she rhapsodizes on creative ambitions: "I don't care what I do so long as it's creative. I want to leave something behind me that was never there before." Henri counters with the reply, "The lavatory's outside."

Later in the film, however, Gosh finds her "creative outlet" by designing the handbag she takes to the front — which, if nothing else, will relieve the tedium of life as a civilian.

Like Shaw, Gosh Boyle is drawn from a real character, a young woman who agreed to sit for Henri but who, after a short time, journeyed to Paris. According to Ede, when she returned, she

> came back with sensational tales of how she danced naked, greatly to the delight of the artists; how Isadora Duncan had wanted to meet her, and how several theatres had offered to engage her. Also Modigliani had wanted to sleep with her, but she had refused because he drank and had no money.

Henri was charmed by her unconventionality and told Sophie that he intended to make love to this woman. Sophie replied that she must be allowed to stand behind a screen when this event took place. Finally, we learn from Ede that after a few weeks Henri brought his model to see Sophie.

> Miss Brzeska was feeling particularly irritated by the noise around her, had stopped her ears with cotton-wool and was sitting right up against the wall, with her back to the room, so as not to see its bare misery, and was singing at the top of her voice.

Russell has Sophie actually set up a screen around the bed ("Take no notice of me") and also uses details from Sophie's actual meeting with Henri's model. The result is an exaggerated and mocking scene, incorporating a number of recurring themes and motifs, such as the "Two Fleas" song, the incomplete sexual encounter, and the strange bond between Henri and Sophie which can't be understood by outsiders.

The use of exaggeration for thematic purposes is by no means the only weapon in Russell's arsenal. The effective use of close-middle shots, the manipulation of setting, and the employment of music for purposes of contrast and allusion are subtle devices rarely noted by reviewers who claim that the film is "very poor technically."

Russell makes extensive use of close-up shots in all his films. In *Savage Messiah*, when filming Sophie and Henri, he often uses the close-middle shot, presenting them together in the frame to suggest visually that they are united against the outside world. When Henri is with Gosh Boyle, Russell rarely includes them in the same frame.

Setting is also used to suggest the pressures of the external world. Only twice do we see the Gaudier-Brzeskas free from the confines of the city. The first is a moment of serenity at the home

of Henri's parents, and the second a moment of grandeur when they journey on holiday to the seacoast. These times, however, are short-lived. The bulk of the film emphasizes the poverty endured by the couple. Russell has often complained that color glamorizes film — even scenes of squalor. While this can be true, his use of lighting and setting at the Putney Arch studio creates an atmosphere of imprisonment.

The open space in front of the arch is a haven for beggars ("If you live in an age of beggars, you must draw beggars") as well as the final resting place for Henri's last unfinished piece of sculpture. Above this area, the iron-barred grating allows a glimpse of the external world: demonstrators against the coming war, cannons on the way to the front in France, and parade bands playing marching songs.

Russell changes the historical Henri's enthusiasm for fighting in the war and suggests instead that society impinges on the artist, who feels that his work is as important as any event occurring in the outside world of politics and social activity. Russell's Henri decides to enlist only after he learns from a newsboy that the Germans have bombed Rheims Cathedral. Although probably the most revolutionary of Russell's artist heroes, Henri cannot totally remove himself from society. Russell emphasizes this fact by a significant shot from the street level down into the basement space as Henri reaches his hand through the grating for a copy of the newspaper.

At the end of the film, Sophie stands alone with Henri's unfinished sculpture in the open space outside the studio, while marching soldiers returning from the war are seen through the outside grating. Thus Russell again shows his viewers the conflict which has been dominant throughout the film.

This conflict is also suggested through the use of music. The forces of conventionality, for instance, are frequently represented by military band music, while a bouncy but dissonant piano accompanies the decadent, bohemian types. Henri and Sophie, on the other hand, are associated with the music of Debussy and, in one particular sequence, the music of Alexander Scriabin. The two spend an afternoon in the country sketching and writing. They look at each other and clasp hands. The long, lingering close-up of the hands — one pair young and smooth, the other thin and worn — is accompanied by the sounds of the opening of the third movement of *The Divine Poem*. This music, according to Scriabin, describes the evolution of the human spirit which, after struggling through intellectual and sexual doubt, reaches a mystical state: "The spirit is now released from its former ties of submission to a higher force . . . it creates its own world by its own creative Will."

This sequence, with its central images of the clasping hands, serves as an aural/visual manifestation of the Platonic link between Henri and Sophie and a necessary prelude to the pledging of troth and the exchanging of last names; but more significantly, it is also part of the film's visual imagery, revealing conflict through contrast. The title credit is set off against Henri's drawing of the bones of a hand, and close-up shots of hands recur in the film — Henri chiseling a stone or sketching, Sophie writing or chopping vegetables, or their hands clasping together. In contrast, we have the bejeweled fingers of Shaw squeezing grapes, the waving hands of Gosh in imitation of a new dance movement, and the hands of the glittering, painted dancers in Shaw's club who cavort about while Corky reads Henri's final letter.

In one of his letters to Sophie, Gaudier-Brzeska states that exaggeration is crucial to artistic truth:

> *In Art one must exaggerate: as the sculptor deepens a depression, or accentuates a relief, so the writer accentuates a vice, diminishes some quality according to his needs; and it is only here that the imagination comes into play. Grandiosity, sublimity and luxury with which you reproach me go with that necessary exaggeration of the facts which helps to secure greater truth, and that is what I mean by a well-thought-out copying of nature.*

Ken Russell approaches the task of adaptation with a similar attitude. Russell is not a translator; he is a transformer of his original sources, and like Gaudier-Brzeska, uses exaggeration "to secure greater truth." Russell is always faithful to what he considers the

Russell directing Antony in **Savage Messiah**

central idea of every situation and character he presents in his films. He uses the facts, the language, the themes, and in some cases even the structure of the literary original, but through his unique combination of these elements, the finding of visual equivalents for verbal conception, and the use of necessary exaggeration, he also manages to present his own personal vision as well.

II. TOMMY

Shortly after leaving the Westbourne Park underground station, I became convinced that I had been misdirected. Kensal Road was not where it should have been according to *London A-Z*; and

Russell working on **Tommy**

this unfashionable West London neighborhood, with its imitation American low-cost housing project and seemingly abandoned large brick buildings, appeared an unlikely location for Lee International Film Studios. A passerby, however, informed me that I was headed in the right direction, and I continued to search for what I imagined to be a massive complex of buildings and location lots surrounded by walls with security guards at the gates. Nothing remotely similar to my expectation seemed possible here, but finally, after walking past "The Lads of the Village" pub, I noticed down the other side of the street a relatively small sign above an entrance way. I was stunned. Lee Studios, with its broken windows

83 /

and dilapidated buildings, looked more like a blitzed-out factory than the site of Ken Russell's offices and studio for his 3.2 million dollar production of the rock opera *Tommy*.

The studio is a short distance from the Russells' home. The modest offices, relaxed atmosphere, and dominant ambience at Lee's, where he made *Savage Messiah* and *Mahler*, enable Russell to have almost the same kind of control and flexibility that he once enjoyed making films for TV. After watching the film crew in action for two weeks, I was struck by the mobility that Russell managed to achieve with a sizeable unit. While film crews at other London studios usually work five days a week from 8:30 a.m. to 5:30 p.m., the crew for *Tommy* worked six days and rarely left before 7 p.m.

According to publicity releases, Russell considers *Tommy* the best opera written since World War II and knew he wanted to make a film version when he first heard the album. But the numerous projects that Russell attempted to bring to fruition after finishing *Savage Messiah* suggest more complicated reasons for his selection of *Tommy*. First, there were plans outside the realm of filmmaking. He was scheduled to direct Peter Maxwell Davies' opera *Taverner*, but finally declined after hearing tapes of a piano and vocal score. Next was an idea, suggested by his wife Shirley, for a stage production about racial conflict in America using elements of opera, ballet, mime and the musical. In the meantime, an adaptation of George Neveux's *Juliette ou la Cle des Songes* was tentatively listed as Russell's next film project. Gradually, however, the Neveux adaptation and Shirley's scheme merged together; and Russell wrote what must surely be his most bizarre script.

The Angels combines, in kaleidoscopic fashion, episodes inspired by the Néveux play, large chunks of material about racial problems, outrageous satire on organized religion and established forms of government, and cryptic autobiographical references. All these concerns are contained within the framework of the film director Michael Mann's "amazing journey" to a film festival in an unnamed East European country. Mann's pilgrimage becomes a mental excursion into the nature of the self and the problems of

Oliver Reed, Roger Daltrey, and Ann-Margret

the artist in the modern world. The film script is a bewildering Kafkaesque nightmare, seasoned with imitations of Fellini's *8½*, and filtered through Russell's unique style and vision.

The most notable aspects of the script concern director Mann's hatred of the fact that early in his career he was forced to com-

The "Lovely Legs Competition" from **Tommy**

promise by making commercials, and those sequences dealing with the religious cult worship which springs up after the supposed death of Mann's big star — Poppy Day, "the Panatella pin up." Poppy's shrine, a satirical jibe at Lourdes, contains a life-size statue of the pop star to which lines of cripples mutter prayers. At the end of the script, Poppy, who has been hiding out in Spain, returns to the shrine.

> *POPPY descends by rope from a helicopter. She lands by her statue. She is dressed identically. She speaks but her voice cannot be heard over the din from the helicopter. She seems to be pleading. A DISILLUSIONED PILGRIM — a young robed man with beard and matted hair throws a stone at her. Others follow suit. ANGY, who at first dropped to her knees, now runs to protect her but is hit by a stone. People are running everywhere. SAMMY is knocked down and trampled to death.*

After MGM turned down this script, in part because they couldn't understand it, Russell began work on *Music, Music, Music* which he described in a *New York Times* interview:

> *The movie will be about the things you have to do for money, from writing music for mad dukes to writing commercials for canned lamb. The artist has always been at the mercy of the commercial, or of somebody who will butcher his work.*

This new film was to carry over some of the same concerns in *The Angels* through the adventures of John Fairfax, the composer of a religious rock opera entitled *Jesus on Venus* — "something that would make *Jesus Christ Superstar* look as old fashioned as a Victorian performance of Handel's *Messiah* among the cast-iron pillars and potted palms of the Crystal Palace." Although the opera is exciting and spectacular, the essence of art, "humanity, love, truth, faith — call it what you will" is missing, perhaps in part because the composer finds it necessary to supplement his income by doing the music for TV commercials. However, after an incident in which a child spews up canned lamb, Fairfax grabs the child and flees from the studio only to be knocked over as he gets outside. When he gets up, he's in the past talking to Johann Sebastian Bach himself. Like Mann in *The Angels*, Fairfax probes into the nature of the self and examines his role as an artist as the result of a metaphorical tour through a history of music which includes the trials and tribulations of Bach and Beethoven and the perversion of established compositions of the past by Hollywood composers like Dimitri Tiomkin. Fairfax abandons the pop religious musical and writes a requiem in which life, death, and resurrection are presented through the songs and street games of school children. John Taverner wrote such a work, and Russell planned to use excerpts to end the film.

After Russell scrapped *Music, Music, Music*, plans were made for *Gargantua*, a screen adaptation of the Rabelais classic to be financed by an Italian production company. The first section of this proposed film revolved around the giant's story presented as a theatrical production; the emphasis was on a merging of various

Daltrey as deaf, dumb, and blind hero

art forms, including song, dance, drama, farce, acrobatics, and burlesque. The remainder of the film, in which the "real" Gargantua appears, contains numerous, often uncomfortably blatant examples of religious and political satire which Russell culled from the scripts of *The Angels* and *Music, Music, Music*. The Italians backed out just before production was about to begin. Then, over a year after the completion of *Savage Messiah*, Russell began work on two projects, a film biography of Gustav Mahler and an adaptation of *Tommy*.

Tommy depicts an episodic passage to self-discovery. According to Russell, the film is structured as "an evolutionary journey" in which the deaf, dumb, and blind protagonist undergoes "a kind of pilgrim's progress" through the horrors of the modern age. The film begins with Tommy's mother and father high atop a mountain at the moment of his conception and closes with an epilogue on the same mountain top years later as Tommy, in "affirmation of Man's eternal divinity," reaches out "as if to embrace the life giving sun."

The climactic scene of the rock opera as conceived by The Who, the revolt of the converts at Tommy's Holiday Camp, bears a remarkable similarity to the dénouement of Russell's *The Angels*. Tommy becomes a space-age Messiah whose followers become disillusioned with him and his message, and the final section of the opera, as Russell interprets it, resembles his abandoned script.

> *They [the converts] feel they've been cheated, sold out, betrayed — they overturn the pin tables, smash the glass and set fire to them. As they did before — in the 'Sally Simpson' number — they storm up to touch the new Messiah, not reverently this time but to batter him. Not least in the forefront of the attack are the Blind . . . Accordingly they belabour him with their sticks. MISTER NORMAL 'puts the boot in,' the DRUNK breaks his bottle over TOMMY'S head . . . FRANK and NORA do their best to protect TOMMY, but the odds are hopeless and they are knocked down and trampled.*

The visuals which accompany the Preacher's (Eric Clapton) rendition of "Eyesight to the Blind" draw heavily on Russell's conception of Poppy Day's shrine from *The Angels*. Only here the life-size plaster statue is of Marilyn Monroe, "one of the great lay saints of the 20th century."

Russell manipulated some of the new material added to the rock opera to express his attitude towards commercial advertising, a major concern in the scripts of both *The Angels* and *Music, Music, Music,* where he savagely attacked commercials which, without our conscious recognition, shape the images that we form of ourselves. Tommy's mother (Ann-Margret), on the verge of a nervous breakdown, sings, "Today It Rained Champagne," while a TV set blares out ads for baked beans, detergents, and chocolates. At the end of the song, she fantasizes that the TV screen splinters into a thousand pieces and a flow of baked beans, face creams, detergents, cigarettes, and chocolates engulfs her bedroom, "like an obscene stream of lava," while the lush music score degenerates into fragments of Rachmaninoff, Tchaikovsky, and Liberace.

Just as the opening of the *Gargantua* project attempted to fuse together various art forms, *Tommy* dispenses with dialogue and merges song, music, mime, dance and visual image in what is possibly Russell's most successful synthesis of the arts — a dream also held by the composer Alexander Scriabin, one of the director's acknowledged influences.

Russell worked for a period of six months with Pete Townshend, composer of most of the songs from *Tommy* and musical director of the film. Together they made slight but necessary alterations to the original lyrics and created six new songs. The shooting script reveals Russell's remarkable success as an adapter-creator who walks a tightrope between his own personal vision and the vital concerns of the work from which the film is made. Although he changed the order of some songs, altered the words of others, and obviously instigated the addition of the new ones, Russell feels that he has remained faithful to the rock opera as conceived by The Who. The problem with the original work, as Russell sees it, rests with the development of the narrative. "It simply jumps into the middle of things and even The Who recognize this as a weakness." As a result, two of the new songs, an instrumental entitled "Prologue 1945" and "Bernie's Holiday Camp," supply the basis for a functional, if somewhat clichéd background. Group-Captain Walker has an idyllic leave with his wife Nora shortly before his plane is shot down over Germany. Some months later on V-E Day, Nora gives birth to Tommy. Six years later at Bernie's Holiday Camp, she meets Frank Hobbs, "your friendly greencoat," falls in love, and later marries him. Captain Walker, a cured amnesia victim, returns home to find Frank and Nora in bed. Walker is killed while the horrified Tommy watches; and as a result of this trauma, Tommy is struck deaf, dumb and blind. (See the script excerpt from *Tommy* in next section.)

Russell carefully revised and reworked the description of the visual action in the 66-page shooting script. These detailed verbal sketches were not fixed blueprints for the film. Russell frequently notes that for him filmmaking is "totally intuitive," but this does not mean that preproduction activities are of little consequence. Instead, it means that he often improvises as he goes along, sometimes as a means of solving the problems that each filming situation poses.

During my visit to the set, there seemed to be endless opportunities for Russell's moments of frustration to boil over into anger, but there were none of those over-publicized outbursts frequently attributed to the director. Sporting an unkempt, silver-grey beard, longish hair, sunglasses, and a candy-striped suit and resembling a cross between Sam Peckinpah and Edmund Gwenn (Kris Kringle in *Miracle on 34th Street*), Russell seemed less the "wild man" described in the press than the hard-working filmmaker who claims that art is 5% inspiration and 95% perspiration.

Some of this perspiration was spent on the shooting of the complex "Acid Queen" sequence in which the Acid Queen (Tina Turner) becomes a modern iron maiden, a combination juke-box and hypodermic. Two handmaidens place Tommy (Roger Daltrey) inside this mechanism. In the shooting script, the doors open to reveal Tommy covered with ants and then as a skeleton "which breaks into a myriad blood-red molecules which whirl crazily about until they form into TOMMY." By the time the actual shooting begins, however, the ants have become caterpillars which are metamorphosed into butterflies, and the molecules are now snakes. The problems of filming these scenes, however, were almost insurmountable. The caterpillars, even when placed in honey or glue, failed to cling to Daltrey's body, and the snakes could not be pushed far enough into the eye sockets of the plastic skeleton. Russell decided to rethink the caterpillar idea and ordered that the back of the skull be opened so that the snakes could be forced through the eye sockets. This necessitated paint to cover the cracks and a slight shifting of the camera angle. The filming process was

Paul Nicholas tries to drown Tommy

long and slow, and an entire afternoon of difficult work often resulted in only a few seconds of usable footage.

Shortly after this frustrating experience, Russell was informed that another of his ideas would have to be altered. He had planned to shoot an eye-level long shot of Tommy smashing through a full-length mirror to "freedom." This was to be accomplished by having Roger Daltrey push through a mirror of ultra-thin glass, but this glass was not being manufactured in any form larger than four feet in length. Some crew members suggested more conventional methods for filming the breaking of the mirror, but Russell, who accepted this bad news without any trace of anger, immediately began working with the manipulation of camera angles and the editing of the shot to achieve something close to the desired effect.

This ability to use imaginatively whatever is available is a major reason why those working for Russell respect him, according to prop men Ron Lewis and Andy Andrews, relative newcomers to the Russell "stock company." Like most of the people working on *Tommy*, they were also on the crew of *Mahler*, which, although shot on a limited budget in an amazingly short period of time, won an award at Cannes for Best Technical Achievement. Other members of the crew, however, like Ian Whittaker, have followed Russell from film to film; and a few, like Shirley Russell and Dick Bush, worked with him on the BBC films.

A kind of "intuitive" bond exists with Dick Bush, director of photography, and with choreographer Gillian Gregory, who replaced Terry Gilbert during the shooting of *The Boy Friend*. Such a relationship with these two people is crucial, since so much of the way in which Russell manipulates the movement of his camera and his actors is indebted to dance. It is not enough merely to describe his camera work as fluid, or to call his nearly non-stop camera movement nonfunctional, as many American film critics suggest. Just as ballet is a dance form employing steps and gestures in flowing, intricate patterns to accompanying music, Russell's camera work creates flowing, intricate patterns to accompany visual action and aural imagery. One immediately remembers the spectacular examples, such as the opening of *The Music Lovers*, but the principle also governs those sequences in a Russell film where there are only a few people in a room.

One of these memorable, less flamboyant moments in *Tommy* occurred during "the Acid Queen" sequence which takes place in "The Sin City Revue Bar." The action is limited — Uncle Frank (Oliver Reed) slips the Acid Queen some money "to take care" of Tommy; it is exactly the kind of scene that another director might simply "throw away." For Russell, however, the light had to be just right, and Tina's swirling movements were blocked out to the slightest gesture. The first takes were interesting enough, but Russell decided to operate the hand-held camera himself. During the next few takes, he moved with the music as he followed the action, and soon the director and the actors were part of a riveting ballet. There was no awkwardness or sudden jerking of the camera — but instead a single, sustaining flowing motion with Russell lunging forward, tilting the camera, sliding back, bending up, and finally capturing that last close-up of Uncle Frank's sinister smile. It was a magic moment illustrating Russell's belief that "what one

Daltrey rehearsing the Pinball Wizard sequence

does with the camera and the way the actors are moved is really choreography."

This method of intuitive filmmaking, however, should not be confused with a chance or haphazard process. As a director who maintains maximum control over the preproduction stage, the actual shooting, and the post-production work, Ken Russell often resembles the brilliant ringmaster of a complex, three-ring cinema circus.

MAHLER
Original Screenplay
by KEN RUSSELL

POST-PRODUCTION SCRIPT
(Opening Scenes)

(Film terminology abbreviations: LS — Long Shot; MS — Medium Shot; CS — Close Shot; MCS — Medium Close Shot; MLS — Medium Long Shot; POV — Point of View; INT. — Interior; EXT. — Exterior.)

LS LAKESIDE HUT. CAMERA ZOOMS IN SLOWLY AND HUT BURSTS INTO FLAMES.

CS MAHLER SEEN THROUGH WINDOW OF COFFEE LID. FLAMES IN FOREGROUND.

SUPERIMPOSITION FADES IN: "MAHLER"

MS ANN VON MILDENBURG. FLAMES IN FG.

MS PUTZI AND GLUCKI SEEN THROUGH FLAMES.

CS ROCK. CAMERA PANS TO ROCK IN SHAPE OF MAHLER'S HEAD. PANS RIGHT TO ALMA IN CHRYSALIS.

MS ROCK IN SHAPE OF MAHLER'S HEAD. CAMERA ZOOMS IN.

MS ALMA CRAWLING ACROSS ROCKS. ALMA CARESSING ROCK.

Russell and actor Robert Powell who plays Mahler

INTERIOR TRAIN. CS PROFILE MAHLER. CAMERA PULLS BACK.

CS PROFILE ALMA.

> ALMA

How do you feel? You dropped off.

CS MAHLER PROFILE.

> MAHLER

Fine. I slept like a log. (Pause.) No, like a rock.

CS PROFILE ALMA.

> MAHLER

The first movement of the Third Symphony kept coming through my head.

Filming **Mahler**

ALMA
"What the rocks tell me." (Pause.) That's because . . . you're conducting it tomorrow.

CS PROFILE MAHLER.

ALMA
You look feverish. Let me take your temperature.

CS MAHLER.

MAHLER
It is nothing to do with my temperature. It's chilly. Close the
window.

MCS ALMA.

MAHLER
And don't fuss. You were part of the dream too.

ALMA
Hm . . . a pebble, I suppose.

MAHLER
No, you were a living creature struggling to be born.

CS MAHLER.

MCS ALMA.

ALMA
At least you've noticed.

CS MAHLER

MAHLER
You were a chrysalis.

MCS ALMA.

ALMA
Ready to turn into a pretty painted butterfly.

CS MAHLER.

MAHLER
Where are you going?

LS ALMA.

ALMA
Oh, just flitting out for a fashion magazine.

LS MAHLER.

EXT. TRAIN. LS ALMA GETTING OUT OF CARRIAGE. REAR VIEW ALMA WALKING DOWN STEPS.

MCS MAHLER SEEN THROUGH TRAIN WINDOW.

MAHLER'S POV. LS BOY IN SAILOR SUIT.

MCS MAHLER SEEN THROUGH TRAIN WINDOW.

MCS MIDDLE-AGED MAN IN WHITE SUIT WATCHING BOY IN SAILOR SUIT.

MCS MAHLER SEEN THROUGH TRAIN WINDOW.

MAHLER'S POV. MAN IN WHITE SUIT AND BOY IN SAILOR SUIT.

MCS MAHLER SEEN THROUGH TRAIN WINDOW.

INT. TRAIN COMPARTMENT. KRENEK SEEN THROUGH WINDOW. HE ENTERS COMPARTMENT.

    KRENEK

Have I the honor of addressing Doctor Gustav Mahler? (Pause.) Siegfried Krenek, journalist, Toblach News. Dr. Mahler, is it true that you cancelled your conducting commitments in New York because the competition from Toscanini was too strong? Or because the people didn't appreciate your own music, or was it simply ill health?

MCS MAHLER.

    MAHLER
I was tired of skyscrapers and sarsaparilla.

MCS KRENEK.

MCS MAHLER.

    MAHLER
I want to find a place near Vienna where the sun shines and the grape grows and I can breathe again.

MCS KRENEK.

    KRENEK
Congestion of the lungs. So it was ill health then.

MCS MAHLER.

    MAHLER
Why is everyone so literal these days? I was speaking metaphorically.

MCS KRENEK.

    KRENEK
Why were you forced to leave the Vienna Opera in the first place? Was it anti-Semitism or because you worked your singers and musicians like a slave-driver?

MCS MAHLER.

    MAHLER
I certainly drove one musician too hard.

MCS KRENEK.

    KRENEK
Dr. Mahler, which do you prefer, conducting or composing?

MCS MAHLER.

    MAHLER
I conduct to live, I live to compose.

MCS KRENEK.

    MAHLER
Now, you have wasted precisely two minutes of my time, Mr.
Krenek. Why don't you do what I do when I'm teaching the New
York Philharmonic to play in time?

MCS MAHLER.

MCS KRENEK.

MCS MAHLER.

    MAHLER
Beat it.

MCS KRENEK.

    KRENEK
(Laughs.) Yes, very good. Thank you, Dr. Mahler. It was certainly
kind of you to talk to me, greatly honored I'm sure. All Austria is
proud to welcome you home again.

MCS REAR VIEW KRENEK DEPARTING.
ALMA ARRIVING.

MCS ALMA.

    MAHLER
Don't say it, I know.

MCS MAHLER.

MCS ALMA.
CAMERA ZOOMS IN TO CS.

INT. MAHLER'S HOUSE.
LS MAHLER FOLLOWED BY ALMA DRESSED AS SHADOW WALK-
ING DOWN STAIRCASE.

LS PROFILE MAHLER & ALMA WALKING DOWN STAIRS.
CROWD APPROACHES AND CONGREGATES AROUND MAHLER.

MLS MAHLER & CROWD APPROACHING CAMERA DOWNSTAIRS.

MS MAHLER SURROUNDED BY CROWDS. CAMERA PANS DOWN
TO LS ALMA ON LOWER LANDING.

INT. TRAIN COMPARTMENT.
CS ALMA.

ALMA

I might as well be your shadow for all the notice anyone takes
of me.

MCS MAHLER.

MAHLER

I was waiting for that. It's about time you changed your tune.

MCS ALMA.

ALMA

Hmm . . . I had plenty of tunes until you killed them all.

MCS MAHLER.

EXT TRAIN. MCS GUARD.

INT. TRAIN COMPARTMENT.
MS MAHLER. TRAIN STARTS.

MAHLER

Right over the wheels and next to the lavatory, you've managed to
reserve the noisiest compartment on the train. (Pause.) Now you
can exert your own personality up to the hilt. Charm the attendant,
seduce him into giving us another one.

ALMA

It was the last one, we were very lucky.

MAHLER

I've got a migraine coming on.

REAR VIEW CS ALMA EXITING.

CS PROFILE MAHLER.

CS ALMA.

CS PROFILE MAHLER.

MCS MAHLER PROFILE.

MAHLER
Privacy, punctuality, and silence, and the greatest of these is silence.

MLS ALMA.

ALMA
But Gustl, it's as silent as the grave.

CS MAHLER.

MAHLER
No dearest, it's as noisy as a nursery. (Pause.) Listen.

MLS ALMA.

LS REVERSE ANGLE.
ALMA AND GUSTL IN HUT.

MS ALMA INT. HUT.

ALMA
But Putzi's asleep. (Pause.) It can't be the children.

CS PROFILE MAHLER.

MAHLER
Listen.

LS ACROSS LAKE.

CS ALMA.

ALMA
(Gasps.) But dearest, they're everyday country sounds. You're teasing. If they really troubled you, you wouldn't write pieces called "What the Animals in the Forest tell me" or "what the flowers in the meadows tell me." Even your titles give you away. All your music is a hymn to nature.

105 /

MAHLER

Not quite all. You have forgotten the most important title. (Pause.)
"What love tells me."

MAHLER

Now give me a hand.

MS TABLE. MAHLER & ALMA ENTER FRAME.

MAHLER

Anyway, I don't want to imitate nature. I want to capture its very
essence, so if all the birds and the beasts died tomorrow and the
world became a desert, when people heard my music they would
still know, feel what nature was.

CS ALMA.

MS MAHLER WALKING LEFT TO RIGHT.

MAHLER

If you really want to help me in my work, run along and see if you
can't stop that racket.

REAR VIEW ALMA LEAVING.

ALMA

When are you going to look at my songs, Gustl? (Pause.) You
promised to ever since we got married.

CS MAHLER'S HAND UP TO FACE.

MAHLER

I know, but I want to study them properly, and that takes time.
When I give up conducting altogether and compose all the time
instead of just during the holidays, it'll be different.

MS MAHLER.

MAHLER

The crows are the worst offenders, and if you can dispose of any
unhatched generations while you're at it . . .

MS ALMA.

> MAHLER
(Offscreen.) You'll save yourself a lot of trouble.

MS MAHLER.

> MAHLER
Close the door quietly as you go.

REVERSE ANGLE CS ALMA.

MS MAHLER INT. HUT.

EXT. MCS ALMA.

INT. HUT MS MAHLER.

MLS ALMA PUSHING PRAM.

Georgina Hale as Alma

Powell and Hale

INT. HUT MS REAR VIEW MAHLER.

EXT. MLS HERD OF COWS.

INT. HUT MS MAHLER.

LS SNOW COVERED MOUNTAINS.

MLS MOUNTAIN PEAK.

CS REVOLVING EARTH.

Directing **Tommy**

TOMMY
A ROCK OPERA
by PETE TOWNSHEND and THE WHO
Screenplay
by KEN RUSSELL

SHOOTING SCRIPT
(Excerpt)

(These pages from the shooting script of Tommy, *with revisions in Russell's handwriting, describe the traumatic event in the hero's childhood that caused him to become blind, deaf, and dumb. Mrs. Walker is Tommy's mother. Captain Walker, presumed killed in the war, is his father.)*

Reed, Ann-Margret, and Barry Winch as young Tommy

Tommy wired up for medical tests

MRS WALKER holds TOMMY in her arms. By the side of the bed a bunch

of flowers. The camera moves ~~into~~ towards them. The petals drop off - only

the skeleton stalks remain. Dissolve through to a single poppy.

Remembrance Day. The poppy is on a small wooden cross in MRS WALKER's

hand. Guns boom. By her side TOMMY stands to attention. The guns

are quiet. The 2 minutes silence is over. MRS WALKER plants her

cross among a thousand similar crosses and kisses TOMMY. Zoom into

crosses and ranks of artificial red poppies. Red fills the screen.

                                                          Dissolve

Red fills the screen. Camera pulls back to show the red jacketed holiday

camp host. He shakes hands with MRS WALKER, pats TOMMY on the head.

The TWO GROWN-UPs look at each other and are attracted to each other.
Ide carries her suitcases to a chalet. Tommy follows behind

LATER. MRS WALKER & the REDCOAT are ~~dancing~~ Smooching together at the camp

dance. TOMMY sits by himself sucking an orangeade through a straw. Later

~~The~~ all three of them leave the camp. Now they are home. MRS WALKER

tucks TOMMY in. The REDCOAT, having discarded his jacket, lurks

discreetly outside the door. On TOMMY's bedside table is the portrait

we saw earlier of CAPTAIN WALKER. Next to it is a model of his

Wellington bomber. MOTHER kisses TOMMY good night and goes out.

TOMMY looks at his father's photograph then closes his eyes. The

room grows dark. CAPTAIN WALKER smiles at TOMMY from his photo frame.

                         beneath
A bar of light appears ~~under~~ the door. The door opens. The figure

of a MAN stands silhouetted in the doorway. He walks towards the bed.

It is CAPTAIN WALKER. Softly, gently, he touches the head of his

sleeping son, tiptoes ~~out and closes the door: click.~~ back to the

door & turns for at last look at Tommy, who

wakes up to see the silhouetted figure a split

second before it closes the door. ~~again~~

Russell explains toy gun to Barry Winch

TOMMY wakes up, sees the light under the door and the shadow of a
figure moving out of the light along the corridor. TOMMY gets out
deserted
of bed, opens his door and creeps along the corridor. His MOTHER's
bedroom door is partially open. Through the crack he sees a flurry
of bodies, sheets, naked flesh - a bedside table lamp raised and
the base brought down in a crushing blow onto his father's head.
At the moment of contact the image freezes for a moment. CAPTAIN
WALKER's agonised face is illuminated with an intense light which
with a clatter of glass
burns everything out before it explodes and plunges the room into
darkness. ~~BLACK.~~

TOMMY blunders down the lit corridor. Screaming silently, blundering
into objects, falling over, getting up, falling over, getting up
and blundering into things again. The LOVER & MRS WALKER come out
of the room, sing:"You Didn't See It", not realising for the moment
that TOMMY is blind, deaf and dumb.

LATER. In an effort to make up for their crime the guilty parties
lavish TOMMY with love and attention but they fail totally either
to
to get through to him or share the secrets of his private world.

Amazing Journey: The FAMILY at the fair. MOTHER & the LOVER take
TOMMY on the dodgems, the 'whip' jungle ride and the Big Dipper.
We share the sensations of the grown-ups. We see the flashing lights,
the swirling vivid colours, the shouts and screams of the riders.
TOMMY knows nothing of this - he feels the sensations of movement
and imagines he is flying through the night sky. Stars burst around
him, spinning him about - or are they imagined explosions of flak
similar to those experienced by CAPTAIN WALKER. Meteors, shooting
stars, flash all around him. In his private flight he smiles a
secret smile.

BIOGRAPHY

Ken Russell was born on July 3, 1927, in Southampton, Hampshire, on the southern coast of England where his film version of Sandy Wilson's musical *The Boy Friend* is set. After attending various local schools, he studied at the Naval College in Pangbourne, Berkshire, and served in the Merchant Navy during the war. He was briefly in the Royal Air Force where he trained as an electrician and directed the camp music circle.

Russell attempted ballet, acting, and then turned to photography. He married the designer Shirley Ann Kingdon in 1957, and they worked together on several of his early short films, among them *Peepshow* and *Amelia and the Angel*. During this period he converted to Roman Catholicism.

On the basis of these films he was hired by BBC-TV as a director, first making short films on the arts for *Monitor* and then progressing to longer biographies of artists and composers for *Omnibus*. Dubbed the "Wild Man of the BBC," Russell became the most famous British TV director of the 1960s. His last BBC film, *Dance of the Seven Veils: A Comic Strip in Seven Episodes on the Life of Richard Strauss*, caused an uproar of controversy when it was telecast in 1970.

Russell's career as a motion picture director has followed a similar pattern of initial enthusiasm from critics, particularly for his *Women in Love* in 1969, and then highly emotional critical abuse for his next films, *The Music Lovers* and *The Devils*. Critical misunderstanding and neglect, however, have not prevented his films from being extremely popular with audiences. Like Hitchcock, Russell is one of the few directors whose name usually guarantees lines at the box office. Recently, many younger directors have acknowledged his influence; and a number of critics have recognized him as among the most imaginative, prolific directors of modern cinema.

Ken and Shirley Russell live with their five children (Xavier, James, Alexander, Victoria, and Toby) in West London near Holland Park in a three-story Edwardian house.

FILMOGRAPHY

Early Films:

PEEPSHOW (1956)
KNIGHTS ON BIKES (uncompleted 1956)
AMELIA AND THE ANGEL (1957)
LOURDES (1958)

Television Films:

POET'S LONDON (with John Betjeman; BBC March 1, 1959)
GORDON JACOB (BBC March 29, 1959)
GUITAR CRAZE (BBC June 7, 1959)
VARIATIONS ON A MECHANICAL THEME (Mechanical musical instruments; BBC September 27, 1959)
Untitled film on painters Robert McBryde and Robert Colquhoun (BBC October 25, 1959)
PORTRAIT OF A GOON (Spike Milligan; BBC December 16, 1959)
MARIE RAMBERT REMEMBERS (BBC January 17, 1960)
ARCHITECTURE OF ENTERTAINMENT (John Betjeman; BBC February 28, 1960)
CRANKS AT WORK (John Cranko; BBC April 24, 1960)
THE MINERS' PICNIC (Brass bands; BBC July 3, 1960)
SHELAGH DELANEY'S SALFORD (BBC September 25, 1960)
A HOUSE IN BAYSWATER (BBC December 14, 1960)

THE LIGHT FANTASTIC (Dancing in England; BBC December 18, 1960)

LONDON MOODS (BBC November 5, 1961)

ANTONIO GAUDI (BBC December 3, 1961)

LOTTE LENYA SINGS KURT WEILL (co-director Humphrey Burton; BBC September 10, 1962)

OLD BATTERSEA HOUSE (Pre-Raphaelite museum; BBC June 4, 1961)

PORTRAIT OF A SOVIET COMPOSER (Sergei Prokofiev; BBC June 18, 1961)

POP GOES THE EASEL (Pop artists; BBC March 25, 1962)

PRESERVATION MAN (Bruce Lacey; BBC May 20, 1962)

MR. CHESHER'S TRACTION ENGINES (BBC July 1, 1962)

ELGAR (BBC November 11, 1962)

WATCH THE BIRDIE (David Hurn; BBC June 9, 1963)

LONELY SHORE (BBC January 14, 1964)

BARTOK (BBC May 24, 1964)

THE DOTTY WORLD OF JAMES LLOYD (BBC July 5, 1964)

DIARY OF A NOBODY (BBC December 12, 1964)

THE DEBUSSY FILM (BBC May 18, 1965)

ALWAYS ON SUNDAY (Rousseau; BBC June 29, 1965)

DON'T SHOOT THE COMPOSER (Georges Delerue; BBC January 29, 1966)

ISADORA DUNCAN, THE BIGGEST DANCER IN THE WORLD (BBC September 22, 1966)

DANTE'S INFERNO (Rossetti; BBC December 22 ,1967)

SONG OF SUMMER (Delius; BBC September 15, 1968)

DANCE OF THE SEVEN VEILS: A COMIC STRIP IN SEVEN EPISODES ON THE LIFE OF RICHARD STRAUSS (BBC February 15, 1970)

Features:

FRENCH DRESSING (1963)

ABPC. Producer: Kenneth Harper. Associate Producer: Andrew Mitchell. Director: Ken Russell. Screenplay: Peter Myers, Ronald

Cass and Peter Brett from original story by Peter Myers and Ronald Cass. Photography: Ken Higgins. Editor: Jack Slade. Costume designer: Shirley Russell. Art direction: Jack Stephens. Music: Georges Delerue.

Cast: James Booth (Jim), Roy Kinnear (Henry), Marisa Mell (Francoise Fayol), Alita Naughton (Judy), Bryan Pringle (The Mayor), Robert Robinson (Himself), Norman Pitt (Westbourne Mayor), Henry McCarthy (Bridgmouth Mayor), Sandor Eles (Vladek).

BILLION DOLLAR BRAIN (1965)

United Artists. Executive Producer: André de Toth. Producer: Harry Saltzman. Director: Ken Russell. Screenplay: John McGrath from

Billion Dollar Brain with Michael Caine and
Francoise Dorleac

Len Deighton novel. Photography: Billy Williams. Editor: Alan Osbiston. Production design: Syd Cain. Art direction: Bert Davey. Music: Richard Rodney Bennett. Production Manager: Eva Monley. Costume designer: Shirley Russell.

Cast: Michael Caine (Harry Palmer), Karl Malden (Leon Newbegin), Francoise Dorleac (Anya), Oscar Homolka (Colonel Stok), Ed Begley (General Midwinter), Guy Doleman (Colonel Ross), Vladek Sheybal (Dr. Eiwort), Milo Sperber (Basil), Mark Elwes (Birkinshaw), Stanley Caine (GPO Delivery Boy).

WOMEN IN LOVE (1969)

United Artists. Producers: Larry Kramer and Martin Rosen. Associate Producer: Roy Baird. Production Controller: Harry Benn. Director: Ken Russell. Screenplay: Larry Kramer from D. H. Lawrence novel. Photography: Billy Williams. Editor: Michael Bradsell. Set Designer: Luciana Arrighi. Costume Designer: Shirley Russell. Music: Georges Delerue. Choreographer: Terry Gilbert.

Cast: Alan Bates (Rupert Birkin), Oliver Reed (Gerald Crich), Glenda Jackson (Gudrun Brangwen), Jennie Linden (Ursula Brangwen), Eleanor Bron (Hermione Roddice), Alan Webb (Mr. Crich), Vladek Sheybal (Loerke), Catherine Wilmer (Mrs. Crich), Sarah Nicholls (Winifred Crich), Sharon Gurney (Laura Crich), Christopher Gable (Tibby Lupton), Michael Gough (Mr. Brangwen), Norma Shebeare (Mrs. Brangwen), Nike Arrighi (Contessa), James Laurenson (Minister), Michael Graham Cox (Palmer), Richard Heffer (Loerke's friend), Michael Garratt (Maestro).

THE MUSIC LOVERS (1970)

United Artists. Executive Producer: Roy Baird. Director: Ken Russell. Screenplay: Melvyn Bragg from *Beloved Friend* by Catherine Drinker Bowen and Barbara Von Meck. Photography: Douglas

Slocombe. Editor: Michael Bradsell. Art Direction: Michael Knight. Production Designer: Natasha Kroll. Set Decoration: Ian Whittaker. Music by Tchaikovsky, conducted by André Previn. Solo pianist: Raphael Orozco. Solo Soprano: April Cantelo. Choreographer: Terry Gilbert. Costume Designer: Shirley Russell. Sound Editor: Terry Rawlings. Production Manager: Neville C. Thompson. Musical Advisers: Michael Moores, Elizabeth Corden.

Cast: Richard Chamberlain (Peter Tchaikovsky), Glenda Jackson (Antonina Milyukova), Max Adrian (Nicholas Rubenstein), Christopher Gable (Count Anton Chiluvsky), Izabella Telezynska "Iza Teller" (Madame von Meck), Kenneth Colley (Modeste Tchaikovsky), Sabina Maydelle (Sasha Tchaikovsky), Maureen Pryor (Antonina's Mother), Bruce Robinson (Alexei), Andrew Faulds (Davidov), Ben Aris (Young Lieutenant), Joanne Brown (Olga Bredska), Imogen Clair (Lady In White), John and Dennis Myers (Von Meck twins), Xavier Russell (Koyola), James Russell (Bobyek), Victoria Russell (Tatiana), Alexander Russell (Mme. von Meck's Grandson), Alex Jawdokimov (Dmitri Shubelov), Clive Cazes (Doctor), Graham Armitage (Prince Balukin), Ernest Bale (Head Waiter), Consuela Chapman (Tchaikovsky's mother), Alex Brewer (Young Tchaikovsky). Georgina Parkinson, Alain Dubreuil, Peter White, Maggie Maxwell (Dancers in *Swan Lake*).

THE DEVILS (1971)

Warner Brothers. Producers: Robert H. Solo and Ken Russell. Associate Producer: Roy Baird. Director: Ken Russell. Screenplay: Ken Russell from *The Devils* by John Whiting and *The Devils of Loudun* by Aldous Huxley. Photography: David Watkin. Editor: Michael Bradsell. Set Designer: Derek Jarman. Art Direction: Robert Cartwright. Costume Designer: Shirley Russell. Choreographer: Terry Gilbert. Music: Peter Maxwell Davies. Period Music Arranged and Conducted by David Munrow. Set Dresser: Ian Whittaker. Production Manager: Neville C. Thompson.

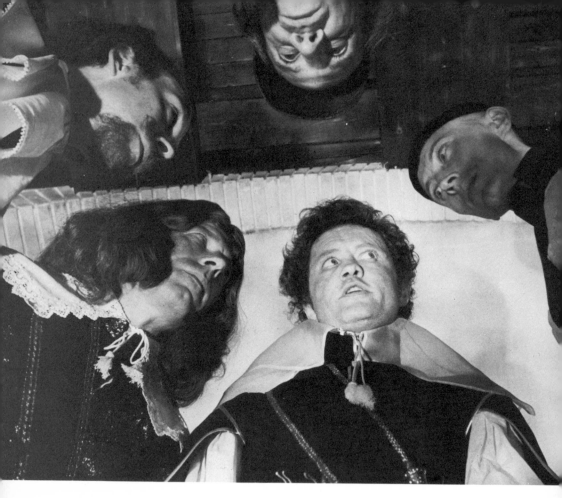

The Devils

Cast: Vanessa Redgrave (Sister Jeanne), Oliver Reed (Father Urbain Grandier), Dudley Sutton (Baron de Laubardemont), Max Adrian (Ibert), Gemma Jones (Madeleine de Brou), Murray Melvin (Mignon), Michael Gothard (Barré), Georgina Hale (Philippe), Brian Murphy (Adam), Christopher Logue (Richelieu), Graham Armitage (Louis XIII), John Woodvine (Trincant), Andrew Faulds (Rangier), Kenneth Colley (Legrand), Judith Paris (Sister Judith), Catherine Wilmer (Sister Catherine), Iza Teller (Sister Iza).

*Christopher Gable and Twiggy in **The Boy Friend***

THE BOY FRIEND (1972)

MGM-EMI. Producer and Director: Ken Russell, Associate Producer: Harry Benn. Screenplay: Ken Russell from Sandy Wilson's musical

"A Room in Bloomsbury" number from **The Boy Friend**

play. Production Associate: Justin de Villeneuve. Photography: David Watkin, Editor: Michael Bradsell. Design Consultant: Tony Walton. Art Director: Simon Holland. Costume Designer: Shirley Russell. Musical Director: Peter Maxwell Davies. Production Manager: Neville C. Thompson. Music Associate: Peter Greenwell. Choreography: Christopher Gable, Gillian Gregory, Terry Gilbert, and members of the cast.

Cast: Twiggy (Polly Browne), Christopher Gable (Tony Brockhurst), Barbara Windsor (Hortense), Moyra Fraser (Madame Dubonnet/ Mrs. Parkhill), Bryan Pringle (Percival Browne/Mr. Percy Parkhill), Max Adrian (Lord Brockhurst/Max Mandeville), Catherine Wilmer (Lady Brockhurst/Catherine), Vladek Sheybal (DeThrill), Ann Jameson (Mrs. Peter), Peter Greenwell (The Pianist), Antonia Ellis (Maisie), Caryl Little (Dulcie), Georgina Hale (Fay), Sally Bryant (Nancy), Tommy Tune (Tommy), Murray Melvin (Alphonse), Graham Armitage (Michael), Brian Murphy (Peter).